The Nineteenth Amendment to the Constitution of the United States of America

"The right of citizens of the United States to vote shall not be denied or abridged by the United States or by any State on account of sex.

"Congress shall have power to enforce this article by appropriate legislation."

Ratified August 26, 1920

A VOICE OF OUR OWN

A VOICE OF OUR OWN

LEADING AMERICAN

WOMEN CELEBRATE

THE RIGHT TO VOTE

Edited by Nancy M. Neuman

Foreword by Becky Cain, President
League of Women Voters of the United States

JOSSEY-BASS PUBLISHERS
SAN FRANCISCO

Substantial discounts on bulk quantities of Jossey-Bass books are available to corporations, professional associations, and other organizations. For details and discount
information, contact the special sales department at Jossey-Bass Inc., Publishers
(415) 433–1740; Fax (800) 605–2665.

For sales outside the United States, please contact your local
Simon & Schuster International Office.

Manufactured in the United States of America.

The chapter titled "Our Collective Challenges" by Donna Shalala is excerpted from a speech
to the National Women's Political Caucus Convention in 1995 and from testimony before the
U.S. Senate Subcommittee on Labor, Health and Human Services, Education and Related
Agencies and is not subject to copyright.

Interior design by Paula Schlosser.

Photography credits are on page 265.

Library of Congress Cataloging-in-Publication Data

A voice of our own: leading American women celebrate the right to
vote / Nancy M. Neuman, editor; foreword by Becky Cain.
    p. cm.
  Includes index.
  ISBN 0-7879-0231-4 (acid-free paper)
    1. Women—Suffrage—United States. 2. Women in politics—United
States. I. Neuman, Nancy M., date
JK1896.V65 1996
324.6'23'0973—dc20   96-1349

FIRST EDITION
HB Printing   10 9 8 7 6 5 4 3 2 1

CONTENTS

BREAKING THE BARRIERS OF DISCRIMINATION

FAMILY, WORK, AND COMMUNITY

FOREWORD

FOR MANY AMERICANS, PARTICIPATION in American democracy
has not always been easy—or even possible. For women, more
than half the American population, the right to vote was won only after
a seventy-two-year struggle.

The essays in *A Voice of Our Own* highlight how far women have
come in the struggle for full participation and equality and, at the same
time, how much remains to be done. Each of the women contributing
to this book offers the reader her unique and often touching perspective on her vision of equality.

The League of Women Voters hopes that women, and men, from
all walks of life throughout the United States and worldwide will not
only find value in the diverse perspectives offered here but also gain a
greater appreciation for the battles that have been fought for many
years, in many arenas, with many weapons, to move women toward

the goal of full participation and equality. By reflecting on the lessons of the past and celebrating our successes, we women can gather our individual and collective strengths to build on those hard-fought gains, to finish the battle.

The league thanks Nancy Neuman, League of Women Voters national president from 1986 to 1990 and professor of women in politics, for so ably leading this effort for the league and editing this collection of significant and personal essays.

It has taken many voices with one vision to achieve an ever increasing role for women in American democracy. *A Voice of Our Own* continues that successful tradition, celebrating who we are and where we are and revealing where we must go.

March 1996

Becky Cain
President
League of Women Voters
of the United States

PREFACE

A T THE CLOSE OF A CENTURY marked by two significant waves of the movement to gain equality for women in America, this collection of essays is a very personal portrait of that struggle. *A Voice of Our Own: Leading American Women Celebrate the Right to Vote* honors the women who came before us and challenges the ones to come. It eloquently expresses the combined experience and vision of women whose leadership inspires and enlightens American society, its culture, and its institutions.

The League of Women Voters commissioned this book in 1995 to commemorate the 75th anniversary of universal woman suffrage in the United States. Itself a product of the woman suffrage movement, the League of Women Voters invited women leaders with diverse life experiences to write for this enterprise. Each was asked, on the occasion of the 75th anniversary, to reflect upon the impact of women's increased political participation and equality on American democracy and to engage the next generation of women.

A *Voice of Our Own* is the result. It is an inspiring conversation about women's lives and women's commitment to improving and nurturing American democracy. It symbolizes the success of the women's movement in the twentieth century and poses questions for the future. A *Voice of Our Own* is the spirited voice of female activism: of young women awakening to public roles, of older women whose battles for equality from the 1930s onward made possible the stories of the women who followed them. The contributors to this book differ in age, background, interests, and political persuasions, but they share at least two important values: that each person has a responsibility to make a difference and that active citizen participation is critical in ensuring that American democracy lives up to its promise of liberty and justice for all.

A *Voice of Our Own* is important reading, especially for women and students of women in American politics and history. It illustrates women's accomplishments in making democracy work, opening up careers and institutions, and becoming politically involved. Even more remarkable is the intensely honest and personal nature of this collection. These stories provide a glimpse of real women living real lives. They have inspired and touched all of us who worked on the book.

Skeptics who pronounce the women's movement dead or dying should read this book. The women in this book *are* the women's movement.

AN OVERVIEW OF THE CONTENTS

Long before winning the right to vote in 1920, American women were active in public life. Former first lady Rosalynn Carter, who generously contributed two essays to this book, first describes the efforts of colonial women to influence the drafting of the U.S. Constitution, and archivist Lucinda Robb discusses presuffrage activism of women at the grassroots. We are reminded that the woman suffrage movement grew out of the antislavery movement in the 1830s and was officially launched in 1848 at the first women's rights convention, held in Seneca Falls, New York.

What did the seventy-two-year struggle for woman suffrage achieve? Antisuffragists and prosuffragists alike oversold the impact of women voting. Like the anti-ERA forces in the 1970s and 1980s, antisuffragists raised the specter of women's equal political rights as a threat to the sanctity of the home; woman suffrage would destroy the American family. Prosuffrage forces insisted that women voting would transform American politics: suffrage would usher in major social reform and clean up corruption.

But millions of women did not vote, and by the mid 1920s, a backlash set in against the reform agenda of the woman suffrage organizations. Not until 1980, sixty years after suffrage was won, did women vote in equal proportions to men. Seventy-five years after suffrage, as journalist Judy Woodruff points out, a record number of women were serving as elected representatives in the United States Congress and state legislatures. Yet compared to men, the proportion of women elected to public office remains small.

The struggle our forebears made to obtain the right to vote is not forgotten. For politician Lindy Boggs, woman suffrage has been a central influence on her entire life. To singer and songwriter Mary Chapin Carpenter, the vote is the emblem of a woman's independence; it is her "pass to the dance." Feminist writer Rebecca Walker will always remember the tears of a ninety-three-year-old woman registering to vote for the first time because a young person cared enough to ask.

Reporter Gwen Ifill and lawyer Antonia Hernández caution us that winning the right to vote has never been sufficient; guaranteeing voting rights for every citizen, especially members of racial minorities, is a continuing struggle that each generation must fight all over again. And nonprofit executive Sara Meléndez questions whether the vote makes any difference at all to women ravaged by poverty.

Winning the right to vote in 1920 did not achieve equality for women. Alice Paul, head of the National Woman's Party, thought an equal rights amendment guaranteeing women and men the same rights under the law should be added to the Constitution. In 1923, when Paul's ERA was first introduced in Congress, a coalition of postsuffrage women's organizations opposed it on the grounds the ERA would eradicate newly won reforms that finally succeeded in regulating hours and conditions of work for women.

This dispute about the ERA, which bore no resemblance to the claims made by anti-ERA social conservatives half a century later, continued for many years, until labor laws changed. Even so, historian and educator Elisabeth Griffith contends that the women's movement has been weakened by the enduring legacy of this division (which she attributes to an even older and bitter schism over tactics that occurred in 1916 between militant suffragist Alice Paul and moderate suffragist and founder of the League of Women Voters, Carrie Chapman Catt).

The debate continues whether women should demand the same treatment as men or different treatment in order to achieve full equality. A recent incarnation of this debate emerged after the deadline to ratify the ERA ran out in 1982. This version celebrates women's "difference" as special, perhaps superior, and a necessary ingredient in all aspects of public life. At the same time, the Family and Medical Leave Act of 1993, which provides identical benefits to women and men and was a priority issue for women's organizations, is a monument to equity, not difference.

In the years between ratification of the woman suffrage amendment in 1920 and the revival of the women's movement in the late 1960s, women and women's organizations did not go dormant. In spite of a backlash against the movement and in spite of the Great Depression and World War II, activist women continued to seek improvement in the status of women.

In the 1930s, Esther Peterson tells us, she learned firsthand about the working conditions women endured in sweatshops, and was motivated to become a labor organizer. Appointed by President Kennedy as assistant secretary of labor and head of the Women's Bureau of the U.S. Department of Labor, Peterson played a major part in enactment of the

Equal Pay Act of 1963, which women's organizations had sought since the end of World War II. Historian Anne Scott's vignette about her own woman suffragist mentors in the League of Women Voters illustrates how involved women were in issues affecting the nation during the war years and the postwar period.

Reporter Sarah McClendon has spent a lifetime working for women's equal treatment. A WAC in World War II, she maintains an active interest in issues affecting the status of women in the military. Businesswoman Barbara Blum begins her essay by recalling the groundwork "Rosie the Riveter" laid during World War II when women performed "men's" jobs, only to be replaced by returning veterans at war's end. Women's roles and opportunities have changed profoundly since then, as Rosalynn Carter explains in her very personal second essay.

A number of pioneers have written essays for this book. Bishop Mary McLeod, the first woman to head an Episcopal diocese in the United States, recounts the pain of discrimination, made all the more hurtful when delivered in the name of religion. Beverly Harvard worked her way up from patrol officer in Atlanta to become the first African American woman to head a police department in the United States. Diane Yu, the first woman, first minority, and youngest person to be appointed general counsel for the State Bar of California, describes growing up in America as the child of Chinese immigrants.

Native American leaders Ada Deer and Wilma Mankiller made history as the first women chiefs of their respective tribes. But Deer's account of Menominee "termination" and Mankiller's description of the suffering Cherokees endured on the Trail of Tears are clear evidence that broken promises are also part of the story of American democracy.

As a new century looms, Health and Human Services Secretary Donna Shalala wonders whether America will renege on its promise to help the poor, the aged, the disadvantaged, and the young. Tennis champion Martina Navratilova yearned to become a U.S. citizen, only to discover that several states would not permit her to apply for citizenship because of her sexual orientation.

Former first lady Betty Ford turned two personal tragedies into opportunities for active work on behalf of women suffering from breast cancer and alcoholism. Physician Bernadine Healy, former head of the National Institutes of Health, issues warnings, particularly to young women, about the potential misuse of scientific advances, especially as they affect women's health and reproduction.

A Voice of Our Own is a call to action. Cartoonist Nicole Hollander offers a unique summons to women everywhere. Activist Maria Luisa Mercado, whose mother was an immigrant Mexican farmworker, considers the kind of future she wants for her daughter. College president Nancy Bekavac warns young women not to take equality for granted or underestimate the hard work that lies ahead. First lady Hillary Rodham Clinton hopes future generations will cease to demean women's rights as somehow separate and less important than all human rights. And Professor Condoleezza Rice cautions us not to forget how far we have come, even as we commit ourselves to perfecting American democratic principles.

ACKNOWLEDGMENTS

For me as editor, this project has been a fascinating journey. Along the way, I could not predict exactly what this book would become—it reshaped itself as each contribution arrived. In the end, however, the combined collection was even better than I had dreamed.

The League of Women Voters is very grateful to the contributors for their thoughtful responses and for the time and energy they contributed to this effort. We especially appreciate their trust: each contributor fashioned her piece without knowing what anyone else would produce. Therefore, these chapters, prepared for this book by invitation, do not represent a consensus of any kind.

My personal deep appreciation goes to President Becky Cain and the national board of the League of Women Voters for believing in the project and inviting me to be the editor. I owe many thanks to Monica Sullivan, publications director, and her assistant Irene Carr in the league's national office for their support, advice, and patience.

And to all the women who struggled to win woman suffrage—those whose names we know and those whose names are known only to their daughters and granddaughters—we thank you!

Lewisburg, Pennsylvania   Nancy M. Neuman
March 1996

A VOICE OF OUR OWN

A VOTE OF
OUR OWN

MARY CHAPIN CARPENTER is a singer, a songwriter, and a multi-platinum-selling recording artist. She is the recipient of five Grammy Awards, two Country Music Awards, and numerous other honors in the entertainment industry. In 1993, she was recognized by the Feminist Majority Foundation for "outstanding work for and commitment to women's equality." In addition to touring and recording, she maintains an active involvement with organizations working on behalf of AIDS awareness, literacy, environmental concerns, and women's issues, among others.

My Vote,
My Self

MARY CHAPIN CARPENTER

A s a songwriter, I have been able to express my thoughts and feelings as a woman, as an artist, and as an American. I have been able to sing about love and the places in my heart where love takes hold. I have been able to write about childhood and certain memories that are points on the compass that guide me toward my forties and middle age. I have been able to observe the lives of friends and strangers and to find the details in our different worlds that connect us.

Songwriting, for me, provides a sense of identity. It allows me to be an individual. Nothing else I do gives me as much self-certitude. It elevates me to a perch from which I am able to develop my perspectives, form my opinions, and craft my personal definitions. I feel my greatest frustration when I am defined by others. I loathe misunderstanding and misconception, yet I find myself in a business that thrives on the definition of people by others. In this way, the music business is a microcosm of our society.

This analogy is further supported by contemporary women, who still find it difficult to seek and establish their own identities. It wasn't so long ago that a woman's reflection was found only in the mirror of her spouse. It wasn't so long ago that a woman who held a job outside the home was frowned upon. Despite the burgeoning numbers of women in the labor force, unforeseen just a generation ago, a woman's worth is still measured differently from a man's. If we "are" what we "do," it's no wonder that a woman's search for identity can be an exhausting and often demoralizing one.

We are still paid less for the same work. We are still passed over for promotions though we hold equal credentials and qualifications. We still endure the impugning language: he is aggressive; she is a bitch. He is ambitious; she is manipulative. He is sensitive; she is overemotional.

Women can gather in any room, on any given day, in any place in America, and exchange similar stories of how these different standards have affected them. But no matter what we do for a living, no matter how distinct our lives are, one fact clearly emerges: we have a powerful, influential voice when we decide that our problems as women in this society transcend party lines. This voice can ensure that there will never be a time in the future when those running for elective office can afford to ignore our concerns. And this singular nonpartisan voice can insist that more of those offices be held by women.

A woman's vote says a great deal about her; it connects her concerns with her beliefs. It reveals her as someone who values and uses her power. Her vote says as much about what she is for as it does about what she is against. It is her calling card, her pass to the dance, her contribution to society. Without the right to vote, a woman was invisible. Now, when she chooses not to vote, she becomes invisible once more. And the voice that can represent the collective concerns of women is diminished as well.

A long time ago, I discovered that songwriting was an antidote for the feelings of disconnection that are such a part of modern life. Like many other women I know, I often feel apart and alone, just trying to find my place in the world. Writing alleviates these feelings and allows me an appreciation of the freedom that this world offers; my right and responsibility to vote results in the same thing. Yet I still need to be reminded from time to time of what I have.

The 75th anniversary of our right to vote is a marker for a struggle and a victory—it defines a passage toward rights and responsibilities. It is an anniversary of a woman's path to identity and empowerment—it is a miraculous thing!

I turned thirty-seven years old in 1995. I look forward to at least another thirty-seven years of living through singing, writing, speaking, shouting, laughing, weeping, protesting, advocating, testifying, loving, sharing, remembering, educating, dreaming, and voting.

There are men and women in our society whom I admire and look up to for their honesty, their compassion, and their commitment to social and economic justice, to support of the arts, to community activism, to diversity, to environmental awareness and action, and to the new ideas that will balance a changing world with our ingrained resistance to change.

I want to demonstrate my faith in these people, and the way I can do it is to cast my precious, treasured one-of-a-kind vote. It will resonate by itself and as a part of a larger chorus. And it will give me as much satisfaction as writing a song that I'm proud of.

GWEN IFILL is a national correspondent for NBC News, based in Washington, D.C. Prior to joining NBC, she worked as a White House correspondent and also covered Congress for the *New York Times*. She spent seven years at the *Washington Post*, rising from an assignment to cover local government in Prince George's County to the national staff. Earlier, she worked for the *Baltimore Evening Sun*, covering city and state politics, and the *Boston Herald American*, where she began her career. She appears frequently on *Meet the Press* and the *Today Show* on NBC and *Washington Week in Review* on PBS. Ifill is a graduate of Simmons College, which awarded her an honorary doctorate of journalism in 1993.

Impact

GWEN IFILL

W HEN I WAS VERY YOUNG, I came home from school one day
to find my big, strong father crying on the couch, sobbing his
eyes out as he watched the news reports about the assassination of President Kennedy.

When I was a little older, I remember snapping on the television
news and watching, transfixed, as a black woman named Melba Tolliver delivered the news. She wore a large Afro. More important, she
reminded me of me.

Early on, I was drawn to the news business for the front-row seat
it offered on world events. I liked to figure out how things worked, and
journalism gave me the constitutionally protected opportunity to be
nosy. Because I considered myself to be serious-minded, I decided to go
into newspapering. This branch of journalism seemed to hold several
advantages. I loved to write but had no patience then (as now) for any-

thing that did not have a built-in deadline. Journalism was for me; long-form fiction was not. I also discovered when I walked into my first newspaper building that I loved the smell of the journalism practiced there. Ink. Newsprint. Photo darkrooms. It all seemed romantic to me.

I worked for seventeen years as a newspaper reporter at four big newspapers, including the *Washington Post* and the *New York Times*. There are few things more fascinating than watching how organizations like this work. Newsrooms contain a wonderful combination of arrogance, absolute certainty about what is important, and nonstop questioning of ourselves and of others.

As in big business, there are few women in positions of power and fewer African Americans. Unlike people in the business world, however, we mostly pretend otherwise. As journalists, we have a responsibility to try to be inclusive in our coverage. And although newsrooms look more representative than they did when I first got into this business nearly two decades ago, they still have a long way to go.

Since 1994, I have worked in television news. I daresay that my reporting and commentary have touched more people in the last twelve months than they have in the last twelve years. An awesome responsibility goes along with the gift of having such impact. I always try to remember that many viewers will never know more about a given issue than I choose to tell them. But I also try to remember that the burden is not entirely on my shoulders. If I, as a young black child, had chosen to form my opinions of myself and base my aspirations on only what I could see in the popular media, I would have despaired of ever accomplishing anything. It was not expected of me by society at large. It was expected of me, however, by my parents.

Yet I carry with me constantly the sense that I have a responsibility to send the correct message to all the little girls who watch me, transfixed, as I watched Melba Tolliver all those years ago.

Impact. It is what we all strive for in our lives. We all yearn to make a difference, whether it is by raising good children, inventing new microchips, or casting the right vote.

Deciding what is—and as important, what is not—news, is about nothing as much as impact.

I love covering politics, and I pretty much like politicians. But the reason I enjoy this form of journalism has less to do with the horse race than with the notion that what politicians do affects people's lives in real ways. Rhetoric has its place, but I was raised to believe that laws and government could change my life in direct ways. I never questioned my right to vote, but as a young news junkie, I was always aware that women and African Americans before me could not take such a right for granted so easily.

Some reporters feel it is a bad thing to vote. They argue that objectivity demands that they reach no conclusions—no matter how privately—about the politicians they cover.

This reasoning collapses for me on two fronts. First, I have never met a reporter who did not reach a private conclusion about a politician she or he was covering. This does not mean that the reporter was not able to cover the politician fairly. It just means that it is the job of reporters to assess the people they cover and reach some sort of conclusion about their character, credibility, and seriousness. Second, I cannot see why I should abstain from exercising an important right and responsibility that was so hard-won.

I think of Bull Connor and hoses. I vote. Simple.

I am often accused of being cynical, but I think I am far from that. It is true that I have little patience for mere grandstanders. But I am always willing to listen to otherwise flawed leaders who at least seem to wrestle with questions instead of just reaching for the obvious, entirely political solution. In the political scheme of things, it seems to me that women have a tougher time being glib in this way. Women are generally too new to the game of political power to allow themselves to be entirely swallowed up in posturing.

When I think about women in Washington struggling for power, I think of Marjorie Margolies-Mezvinsky. She was the first-year member of Congress from Pennsylvania who risked her political livelihood on a Clinton administration budget bill. She voted for it. She was literally booed on the floor of the House. And she was booted out of her congressional seat in the next election. We will never all agree whether or not she was right on the merits. What is unchallenged is that she took an act of unusual political courage. And she paid a price.

In journalism, too, we pay a price for the chance to ask the questions at White House news conferences, for the opportunity to say out loud what most people can only mutter at their television screens. And we take a lot of criticism. So be it. When it comes to my work, my hide is pretty tough. If I cannot defend what I say or what I write, I probably should be keeping it to myself.

When I worked in newspapers, it was always instructive to read through the mail, even when it was written sideways or pasted together out of magazine cutouts. Much of the exchange was thoughtful, often challenging, and never boring. Interestingly, I get less mail in television. I imagine people usually "write in" with their remote control pads. But recently, my faith in the art of correspondence was restored. I appeared on *Meet the Press* in a discussion about race. And one viewer, Margie Love of Ogdensburg, New York, took the time to write me a long, thoughtful letter about her reaction to the program. She described herself as a "white, middle-aged housewife" who experienced "culture shock" when she was first exposed to discrimination based on race. She said she finds it hard to believe that racism is as widespread now as she is generally led to believe from watching television news.

"We all have our own truths," she wrote. "But some truths are universal, and it is upon those that we must all strive to find common ground, and try to overcome the differences rather than constantly condemning our entire society as basically degenerate and evil."

I was heartened by this letter's reasoned tone. It restored some of my faith that the impact we strive for in television is sometimes well received. We seem to hear little of this sort of exchange anymore, so I found Mrs. Love's letter refreshing. In an era of talk-show democracy, much informed political debate has been replaced with shouting matches. They may be vastly entertaining, but I seldom come away having learned very much.

Talk shows can be a wonderful component of open exchange in a free society, but I fear they often degenerate into a forum for heat rather than light. My pet peeve is that people have confused what journalism is all about. They equate Rush Limbaugh, Oprah Winfrey, and Sally Jesse Raphael with Ted Koppel, Tom Brokaw, and Jane Pauley. I shouldn't have to argue that this is a specious notion. But I often have to. And when I do, I am yet again reminded of the responsibilities that come with having impact.

Oprah Winfrey is no journalist, but I applauded her when she said she no longer wanted to use her program as a platform for popular dysfunction. Journalists have the same responsibility. I like to believe that we stand a better chance at presenting balanced reports and having a beneficial impact when we have news staffs that are more representative of our varied society. That way, we are more likely to have people delivering our news who know what it is to think differently from the pack, people who remember what part the press can play in maintaining a vital democracy.

With any luck, journalism can emerge from the 1990s with its reputation for fairness and thoroughness intact.

And maybe we will then also be able to command the same respect journalists commanded when I was a little girl and believed every single thing Chet Huntley ever said.

REBECCA WALKER founded Third Wave Direct Action Corporation after she graduated from Yale University in 1992. As its first major project, this national nonprofit organization devoted to cultivating young women's leadership and activism registered over 20,000 new voters in inner cities nationwide. Named one of the fifty future leaders of America by *Time* magazine in 1994, Walker is the editor of *To Be Real: Telling the Truth and Changing the Face of Feminism* (1995), an anthology exploring young women's relationships with feminism in the 1990s, and a contributing editor to *Ms.* magazine.

Finding America

Rebecca Walker

W HEN MY COLLEAGUE Shannon Liss and I decided, in the summer of 1992, to rent three buses, fill them up with a motley
crew of folk of every persuasion, and drive around the country registering people to vote, we had no idea what we were getting ourselves into.

Responding to government-sanctioned police brutality and sexual
harassment, epitomized at the time by the Rodney King verdict, the
Anita Hill–Clarence Thomas debacle, and the legislative attacks on
Roe v. *Wade,* we knew that we wanted to see the election of a new
administration. Troubled by the ubiquitous accusation that our generation was apathetic and apolitical, we knew that we also wanted to
cultivate and demonstrate young people's leadership by advocating the
involvement of young people, and especially young women, in the
democratic process.

Because we believed that the process by which we did this mattered just as much as the product, we wanted the trip to be as diverse as humanly possible, so that people from different backgrounds would have an opportunity to know and care about each other in an environment less charged and more equality driven than the "real world." By the time we had our 125 Freedom Riders boarded on three video-equipped buses and gave interviews to MTV and Channel One in New York, we knew just a little more.

We knew what it was like to raise $150,000 (exhausting and often humiliating) and what it meant to bring people of many different backgrounds together (stressful and exhilarating). We knew how to negotiate for better deals for everything from hotel rooms to bullhorns (be prepared to walk away), how to garner in-kind donations of food, shelter, and even condoms (ask for them in exchange for a public mention), how to present relevant voting statistics and our message to The Media (speak clearly and carry a Big Name), and—probably most useful—how to get through steering committee meetings, where everything was or was not decided and where power was questioned and struggled over constantly, without having nervous breakdowns (have the meetings over food and keep them short).

What we still didn't know after weeks of intense round-the-clock organizing, and what no amount of planning could ever approximate, was the state of our huge nation. How would North America look and feel to our diverse and idealistic posse? And perhaps even more germane, how would the gritty "real world" receive us? Could we really make the kind of profound impact on our government and communities that we hoped for? Could we really be changed as individuals by the experience?

These are the questions many of us were asking more than one hundred years after the Emancipation Proclamation and almost seventy-five years after woman suffrage, at a time when, though enfranchised and eligible, more than half of the nation's population skipped the voting booth on election day, opting out of the process that could affect their lives dramatically. These are the questions we asked as we sped by the hundreds of prefabricated "housing units" along the highways and byways of the country and the corresponding hundreds of Arby's/Wendy's/Taco Bell/Pizza Hut/McDonald's/Burger King/Dairy Queen strips that serve as Town to so many of America's counties. These are the questions we asked as we listened to some of our youngest Riders recount their experience of being trapped in gang cross fire while registering voters in south central Los Angeles and as we met the many, many disillusioned citizens who refused to register, often adding pointedly, "What good is registering going to do *me?*"

Fortunately, our questions were answered again and again by real people around the country, like the women of the Black Women's Political Action Committee in East Cleveland, one of the hardest hit inner-city communities in the country, who met our buses in the middle of night with huge smiles and plates of steaming food they had been preparing since noon. After eating, showering, and sleeping with us, they accompanied our group to nearby housing projects so tough that community leaders insisted we be escorted by city police. Reminding me of my staunch and opinionated aunts and grandmothers, these women embraced our group with the unwavering support of family and affirmed for all of us that what we were doing was helpful even if it only raised people's spirits and their expectations of what young people could do.

Also affirming were people like the ninety-three-year-old woman in Greenwood, Mississippi, who cried as she filled out the prohibitively complicated Mississippi registration form because no one had ever asked her to vote before, no one "had ever thought my little voice was worth anything." And the older white women with Big Hair and Big Nails who smoked long skinny cigarettes in Lubbock, Texas, who I am sure were Republican and who couldn't have thought too highly of our multi-culti "Silence = Death" T-shirt-wearing Riders. They supported our mission to further democratize our nation by meeting our buses with huge platters of fried chicken and big red coolers full of Kool-Aid. Observing cautiously but not talking to or getting too close to any of us initially, they later shocked me by lining up to give warm goodbyes to the Riders as we left, calling for us to "be sure to come back next year." We had won these seemingly conservative women over, dreadlocks, pierced tongues, Ivy League diplomas, and all.

By the end of the twenty-three-day twenty-one-city journey, it was clear by all quantifiable standards that the trip was a success and that we had made a profound impact. We had registered more than twenty thousand new voters in inner cities across the country and encouraged countless others to vote through the local and national media. The Riders, though exhausted and full of opinions about what went wrong on the trip, made lasting bonds with people they would never have met ordinarily and went home with the great satisfaction of having done something for the greater good. A new national young women's organization had been successfully launched, and young women who wanted to participate were writing and calling us from all over the world.

But perhaps the most valuable outcome of the trip, and this is one of those visceral, almost intangible measures of success, was the understanding that I and many others came to about the nature of pluralism. Because the Riders worked, ate, and slept together twenty-four hours a day, with no privacy and few opportunities to break away from the larger group, the buses were like a hyper-intense mini-America on wheels, a crash course in and test of the principles this country is supposed to be based on. We were forced to grapple with how difficult it is to treat each other equally and with respect, no matter how alien or offensive or utterly disturbing we might find one another.

This was especially hard when physical and psychological safety was at stake. How would we deal with the very disturbing male Rider who threatened to cut off the hands of a female Rider? What would we do about the offensive male Rider who allegedly grabbed the breast of one of our youngest female Riders? How could disputes rooted in a general socially cultivated discomfort with racial and other cultural differences be resolved? How could we work proactively to break down deeply held assumptions about one another in order to coexist, if not in harmony then at least in relative peace?

In one particularly banal but significant episode, one white Jewish member of Group Six was overheard telling one of her white non-Group-Six friends that though she wanted to watch a Spalding Gray movie on the bus, she didn't think that her groupmates (three Muslims, one community organizer, and one recovering crack addict—all African American) would be "interested." One of the black women confronted her, accusing her of assuming that her groupmates were not intellectual enough to appreciate Spalding Gray because of the color of their skin. The white woman denied any such thing, explaining that because no one in her family ever wanted to watch Spalding Gray (they found him too dry), she just assumed that other "normal" people wouldn't want to either.

By the time my company was requested by a bus leader, this exchange had become a tense "situation," dividing the bus into two hostile camps, literally the blacks, who "happened" to be sitting at the back of the bus, versus the whites, who "happened" to be sitting toward the front. Many miles and one group therapy session complete with tears and awkward silences later, the white woman finally acknowledged that what she said could be perceived as racist. The African American women accepted this as an apology, while saying that they could see how she might not have meant to be dismissive or insulting. This process took the better part of a day, or more aptly, the better part of Wyoming to Wichita.

While asking the two guys who were threatening other Riders to pack their bags and board the next train to New York was logistically complicated and an exhaustive test of the leadership's judicial powers, the hard work of encouraging what felt like warring factions to validate the perspectives and thus the humanity of one another was the true hero's journey. It reminded us that voting is indeed key to upholding the ideal of pluralism but nothing compared to the work we will all have to do, with others and on ourselves, to live peaceably with diversity.

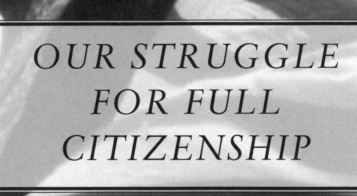

OUR STRUGGLE
FOR FULL
CITIZENSHIP

ROSALYNN CARTER was first lady of the United States from 1977 to 1981. Today she continues to advocate for mental health, early childhood immunization, human rights, conflict resolution, and the empowerment of urban communities through her work at the Carter Center in Atlanta, Georgia. She is a graduate of Georgia Southwestern College, which honored her in 1987 with the establishment of the Rosalynn Carter Institute, a nonprofit organization to help family and professional caregivers. She is a Distinguished Fellow at the Emory University Institute for Women's Studies and serves on the boards of the Friendship Force, Gannett Company, Habitat for Humanity, and the Menninger Foundation. She is the author of three books—*First Lady from Plains* (1984), *Everything to Gain: Making the Most of the Rest of Your Life* (1987), and *Helping Yourself Help Others: A Book for Caregivers* (1994).

Women Who Shaped
the Constitution

ROSALYNN CARTER

*I*N 1987, OUR COUNTRY began a five-year commemoration of the
bicentennial of the United States Constitution. It was a significant
anniversary. Chief Justice Warren Burger resigned from the Supreme
Court to preside over the celebration. Many events were planned in
communities all across the country. One particularly remarkable event
took place in Atlanta, Georgia. Some 2,000 people gathered for a symposium that drew representatives from all fifty states and ten foreign
countries. Included were more than 150 of the most outstanding scholars on women's issues as well as many of the best-known women leaders in our country today. All were part of a symposium called *Women
and the Constitution: A Bicentennial Perspective.*

For more than a year and a half, we at the Carter Center, in con-
junction with Emory University, Georgia State University, and the

Jimmy Carter Library, planned the event. I met with former first ladies Betty Ford and Lady Bird Johnson at the LBJ Ranch in the summer of 1987 to discuss the plans, and although she couldn't be with us, Pat Nixon agreed to join in the effort as a coconvener.

Women have always been a powerful force in our country, even in the earliest years of its history, yet oftentimes they have remained invisible. The names of our forefathers come readily to mind. But what of the women? Our symposium participants posed, and I think answered, the question long overlooked by our society: What roles have women played in shaping the Constitution of the United States, and what impact has that document had on women?

REVOLUTIONARIES

When the Founding Fathers met in Philadelphia in 1787 to draft the Constitution, they did not have women's rights on their minds. They did not grant women the right to vote or a voice in the government that was being formed. There was a simple reason for this neglect: both the Constitution and the Bill of Rights were based on an eighteenth-century concept of justice and equality that was an exclusively white, male system of law and order. The Founding Fathers were simply the patriarchal products of their time.

The prevailing thought of the day was that the American voter must be independent and uncoerced. Men without property could not be independent and uncoerced because they were vulnerable to their landlords. Married women were subject to their husbands' wishes, so it followed that they could not be independent voters. Under this reasoning, one would think that unmarried propertied women would have the vote, but as John Adams said, "you have to draw the line somewhere!"

Our Constitution was not perfect when it was signed; it is not perfect today. But our forefathers had the wisdom to make it possible for us to amend it. Thus, even without formal constitutional rights and lacking the right to vote throughout most of our history, the influence of women on the constitutional process, from the beginning, has been significant.

Who are these invisible women who struggled to protect our rights—or to demand them? They need to be remembered so they can be institutionalized as contributors to our democratic heritage.

Abigail Smith Adams is one of the few women of the eighteenth century who has remained in the public eye. There are several reasons for the continued interest in her life. Hundreds of the letters she wrote over her lifetime were preserved by her family. She also lived during an important era of American history and was related to famous men. Her husband, John Adams, was one of the founders of the nation and the second president of the United States. Her son, John Quincy Adams, was the sixth president, as well as a diplomat and member of Congress for more than two decades.

Abigail was a woman of her times and believed that a woman's role was domestic. But she was intelligent, self-educated, and articulate and could understand and comment upon political issues, as her letters show. And although she did not shape her husband's policies, her correspondence with him, as illustrated in the following excerpts, informs us of the desire of some women of that period to be included in affairs of state.

Abigail Adams to John Adams, as he sat at the Second Continental Congress, March 31, 1776.

[I]n the new code of laws which I suppose it will be necessary for you to make, I desire you would remember the ladies and be more generous and favorable to them than your ancestors. Do not put such unlimited power into the hands of the husbands. Remember, all men would be tyrants if they could. If particular care and attention is not paid to the ladies, we are determined to foment a rebellion, and will not hold ourselves bound by any laws in which we have no voice, or representation.

John Adams in response to Abigail, April 14, 1776.

As to your extraordinary code of laws, I cannot but laugh. We have been told that our struggle has loosened the bonds of government everywhere; that children and apprentices were disobedient; that schools and colleges were grown turbulent; that Indians slighted their guardians, and negroes grew insolent to their masters. But your letter was the first intimation that another tribe, more numerous and powerful than all the rest, were grown discontented. . . . Depend upon it, we know better than to repeal our masculine systems. . . . We have only the name of masters, and rather than give up this, which would completely subject us to the despotism of the petticoat, I hope General Washington and all our brave heroes would fight.

One woman who did influence the thinking of the day when the Constitution was being written was Mercy Otis Warren. She was born into a politically prominent family in Massachusetts, and at a time when other females were learning flowery letter writing, she was sharing her brother's Harvard College classwork. She married a Massachusetts legislator who encouraged her involvement with public affairs, and she was known by most of the framers and founders of the Constitution, including George Washington, Benjamin Franklin, Samuel Adams, John Adams, and Thomas Jefferson. She corresponded with them about social and political issues, the ideals and ideas of the day.

During the growing protest among the Colonies against British rule, Warren and her husband were part of a small circle of patriots, including Samuel Adams, John Adams, and John Hancock, who met in their homes to exchange ideas about forming a government for this new country, debating the structure, function, and processes of colonial, confederate, and constitutional governments.

Although she never strayed far beyond Boston, Mercy Warren's extensive correspondence, satirical plays, poetry, and anti-Federalist tracts were read and discussed in all the states and in Europe. Her writings reflected on the very essences of liberty and democracy as she argued for the complete protection of human rights. She influenced the language of the Constitution even though she was not allowed to be

present at the convention that adopted it. Influenced by her reading of
John Locke and other Enlightenment philosophers, Warren once wrote
that "man is born free and possessed of certain unalienable rights"—a
principle now etched in the Declaration of Independence.

WOMAN SUFFRAGISTS AND THE CONSTITUTION

During the first half of the nineteenth century, American woman suffragists, in an attempt to make their voices heard, worked mainly
through the abolitionist and temperance movements. Three of the
prominent women who participated early in the movement were Lucretia Coffin Mott, Elizabeth Cady Stanton, and Susan Brownell Anthony. Antifeminist prejudices were so prevalent, however, that their
roles were severely limited. A notable instance of the barriers these
early feminists faced occurred at the 1840 Anti-Slavery Convention
held in London. For several days, the convention debated bitterly the
right of eight American women to take their seats as delegates. Internationally famous clergymen contended that equal status for women
was contrary to the will of God. (How familiar to those of us who
worked for the Equal Rights Amendment!) Eventually the women were
permitted to sit behind a curtain, effectively shielded from view and denied the right to speak.

After many such rebuffs, Mott and Stanton decided that the rights
of women, as well as those of black slaves, needed to be ensured in the
Constitution. They decided to create a separate movement dedicated
solely to women's rights. In July 1848, they organized the first women's
rights convention, held in Seneca Falls, New York. For this convention,
Stanton drafted the Declaration of Sentiments, declaring that "men and
women are created equal." She proposed a resolution demanding—for
the first time in public—voting rights for women.

Many citizens and the great majority of newspapers responded
with ridicule, fury, and vilification. Suffragists were called the "shriek-
ing sisterhood," branded as unfeminine, and accused of immorality and

drunkenness. Later, when suffragist leaders undertook speaking tours in support of women's rights, temperance, and abolition of slavery, their speeches were often stormed and disrupted by gangs of street bullies. On one occasion when Susan B. Anthony spoke in Albany, New York, the city mayor sat on the rostrum brandishing a revolver to discourage possible attacks by hoodlums in the audience.

Susan B. Anthony's work for women's rights began in 1851 when she met Stanton. It was the beginning of a fifty-year collaboration for feminist causes. For a time, Anthony and Stanton concentrated on reforming New York State laws discriminating against women. But they soon became convinced that women would not gain their rights or be effective in promoting reforms until they had the vote, and after the Civil War, nationwide suffrage became Anthony and Stanton's goal. In 1869, the two feminist leaders created the National Woman Suffrage Association to work for a constitutional amendment giving women that right.

In 1872, about 150 women across the country tried to vote in the presidential election in order to test the citizenship guarantees of the newly ratified post–Civil War 14th and 15th Amendments to the Constitution. In her hometown of Rochester, New York, Susan B. Anthony went to a barber shop that served as a polling place, and convinced two out of the three polling inspectors to register her. By the end of the day, twelve more women had registered. Anthony and the other women then voted in the presidential election.

Two weeks later, Anthony was arrested and, while awaiting trial, engaged in highly publicized lecture tours. When convicted, she refused to pay her bail, hoping to force the case to the Supreme Court to test the 15th Amendment, which she interpreted as enfranchising American women as well as male ex-slaves. The judge, apprehensive that she might appeal to higher courts, allowed her to go free. Her friends were never brought to trial.

However the case of another early feminist did go to the U.S. Supreme Court. Virginia Minor, who was president of the Woman Suffrage Association of Missouri, had attempted to vote in St. Louis in

1872. When the registrar refused to permit her to register, she and her husband, Francis, an attorney, sued him for denying her one of the privileges and immunities of citizenship expressed in the 14th Amendment. When they lost the case, they appealed to the Supreme Court, which ruled against Minor, stating: "For nearly ninety years . . . uniform practice long continued had settled the question that when the Constitution conferred citizenship, it did not necessarily confer the right of suffrage. . . . Our province is to decide what the law is, not to declare what it should be" (*Minor* v. *Happersett,* 1875).

The decision of the court meant that woman suffrage could not emerge from reinterpretation of the Constitution; it would require either an explicit constitutional amendment or individual revisions of laws in each state.

Anthony's ordeal and the Supreme Court decision energized the women's movement. In 1876, Stanton, Anthony, and three other leaders of the National Woman Suffrage Association staged a demonstration in Philadelphia at the centennial celebration of the Constitution. Prohibited from taking part in the official proceedings, they distributed copies of their own Women's Declaration of Rights to the crowd.

In 1890, the American Woman Suffrage Association, which had been working to change laws state by state, merged with the Stanton-Anthony group to form the National American Woman Suffrage Association (NAWSA). Led by feminist Lucy Stone, the "American" group had long disagreed with the "National" group about whether the campaign to win suffrage should be conducted at federal or state levels. The merged NAWSA worked for many years thereafter to advance women's rights on both state and federal levels. Largely as a result of agitation by NAWSA, suffrage was granted to women in a number of states in the late 1800s and early 1900s.

The women's movement scored its climactic victory shortly after the end of World War I. On June 4, 1919, Congress approved the 19th Amendment to the U.S. Constitution, providing that "the right of citizens of the United States to vote shall not be denied or abridged by the United States or by any State on account of sex." Later ratified by the necessary thirty-six state legislatures, the 19th Amendment became the law of the land on August 26, 1920—133 years after the Constitution was drafted!

EPILOGUE

American women have played and are continuing to play a vital role in the history and development of the Constitution. They have worked and fought against enormous odds in order to ensure the rights all American women now possess. I have written about only a few of them here.

Those of us who attended the *Women and the Constitution* symposium in Atlanta studied and documented the lives of many remarkable women who were ahead of their time, some who are the most accomplished women of today. We also discussed the constitutional issues that affect us every day—at home, on the job, and in our roles as executives and homemakers, caregivers and pathfinders, pioneers and peacemakers.

Drawing upon the symposium materials, the Carter Center has published a four-volume set of educational materials for secondary school courses. The set includes a collection of the major symposium speeches and addresses, a student textbook with an accompanying teacher's guide, and a book of the symposium papers. The set is designed to be the principal material for a program in women's studies, and it can also be used to enrich courses in civics, American history, and American government.

The Student Textbook and *Teacher's Guide* are both authored by Marjorie Wall Bingham, one of the country's foremost women's studies curriculum writers. The essays in *The Symposium Papers* were written by outstanding scholars and by individuals who have direct experience of specific situations involving women's issues. Among these papers can be found, for example, Johnnetta B. Cole's "African Women: Education and Two Hundred Years of the Evolution of the United States Constitution," and "With All Deliberate Speed," the contribution of Leola Brown Montgomery, whose daughter Linda was the plaintiff in *Brown* v. *Topeka Board of Education,* the landmark 1954 Supreme Court school desegregation case. *Speeches and Addresses* contains words that are as timely today as they were when spoken, such as Sandra Day O'Connor's observation that "despite the relative gains women have made over the last 30 years . . . there are still significant gaps" or Geraldine Ferraro's admonition that "if you don't run, you can't win."

These materials are available through the Upper Midwest Women's History Center at Hamline University in St. Paul, Minnesota. The Carter Center has also donated a complete set of the volumes, research papers, and videos of the proceedings to the Jimmy Carter Presidential Library and to the National Archives to make them more accessible to the public.

I look back on the *Women and the Constitution* symposium as an important effort to create for our children a legacy of women's contributions in law, economics, political science, and sociology during the first two hundred years of our country. And when this nation celebrates the tricentennial of the Constitution, this knowledge will be available to them. I hope it will be taught as part of our history and become familiar to our children for generations to come.

LUCINDA DESHA ROBB serves on the outreach staff at the Center for Legislative Archives at the National Archives where she is project director of *Our Mothers Before Us: Women in Democracy, 1789–1920*. Her first major project was *A Splendid Misery: The Presidency of Thomas Jefferson*. She formerly worked at Walt Disney World. She has been a volunteer for Reading for the Blind, the Washington EAR, Girl Scouts of America, and Give Kids the World. She is a trustee of the Fairfax County Public Library Foundation and editor of a political networking newsletter for the Good Ole Girls Network of Virginia. A graduate of the Woodrow Wilson School of Public Affairs at Princeton University (1990), Robb has backpacked through Turkey, Kenya, Brazil, Madagascar, South Korea, Botswana, Zimbabwe, Argentina, Chile, Morocco, Cambodia, and Vietnam and has a fairly good PEZ collection.

Lessons from the Woman Suffrage Movement

LUCINDA DESHA ROBB

I HAVE BEEN WORKING since 1994 with a team of archivists and volunteers on a project called *Our Mothers Before Us: Women and Democracy, 1789–1920,* which highlights women's writings to Congress in the years before women had the right to vote. Sifting through some 20,000 cubic feet of legislative records, we have unearthed extensive evidence of the political involvement of women long before they had the right to vote.

The letters, telegrams, pictures, maps, political cartoons, and petitions we have from such famous American women as Susan B. Anthony, Clara Barton, and Harriet Tubman collectively tell the story of women's perseverance and civic responsibility. From first lady to former slave, from individuals to organizations thousands strong, these petitioners reflect the diversity of women's participation in American democracy.

Being the director and chief cheerleader for *Our Mothers Before Us,* I do a fair amount of public speaking about the project, especially to women's groups. Often when I try to explain about women's early political activity, I get a sort of surprised look. "In our grandmothers' day," people say to me, "it was different. Women couldn't do any of the things that they can do now." It is a common misconception that the women's rights movement began in the 1960s and that before that women just hung around the kitchen, barefoot, pregnant, and oppressed. It is a shame that so much of women's history has been forgotten, for there is not only a rich tradition of women's political participation to be proud of but also much we can learn from the women of the past.

It may be a tired cliché that history repeats itself, but you can't work at the National Archives and not realize just how true the cliché is. Everything I have read about woman suffrage, from the successful campaign strategies to the critical mistakes, seems relevant to the modern women's rights movement. The length of the woman suffrage struggle, the variety of issues, personalities, and ideologies it encompassed, and the fact that it stretched through two major wars, sixteen presidents, and disparate political climates means that it contains a precedent for just about any issue confronting the modern-day feminist.

Through their letters, newspaper clippings, speeches, petitions, and histories, the suffragists left a legacy that is more than just a source of great quotes. Their records offer a guide at a time when the modern-day women's movement could use some direction. The following are just three of the lessons of the woman suffrage movement that seem to me to have a particular relevance to the present day.

WOMEN'S VIEWS ARE ALL OVER THE POLITICAL SPECTRUM

It is tempting to hypothesize that women are more uniform and monolithic in their opinions than they really are. Much of the difficulty in trying to define a "women's political agenda" comes from the fact that women can be located all over the political map. This idea was brought home to me when I started reading through the petitions and letters opposing woman suffrage. While huge numbers of women worked to get the vote, a significant number of women not only opposed suffrage but worked actively to defeat it.

It startled me to learn that these antisuffrage women were not self-loathing troglodyte puppets. While many of the women who worked against suffrage were upper-class socially prominent "conservative" women (none of which makes their opinions any less valid), some of these same antisuffrage women were also challenging the status quo and creating new roles for women. The antisuffrage ranks included the celebrated muckraker and Standard Oil nemesis Ida Tarbell, women's education advocate Catherine Beecher, and prison and insane asylum reformer Dorothea Dix. Union organizer "Mother" Jones thought the struggle for suffrage was a waste of time that kept women from focusing on the real issues of economics. The first woman lawyer, Phoebe Couzins, started out working for woman suffrage and then, to the enormous dismay of Susan B. Anthony and others, changed her mind and came out against it! Even the venerable Lucretia Coffin Mott, one of the Founding Mothers of the women's rights movement, originally had doubts about the wisdom of seeking the vote.

Arguments set forth by the Massachusetts Association Opposed to the Further Extension of Suffrage to Women are representative of the feelings of many antisuffragists. Along traditional lines, the association argued that the most important influence a woman can have is as a wife and mother. Not having a very high opinion of the political process, the association's members also did not want to be corrupted by it, as they thought women surely would be if they became politically involved.

Like the suffragists, however, many antisuffragists took great pride in the accomplishments of women and lauded their work as reformers. To them, the limitation of women's political activity was not a constraint; it was a virtue that allowed women to advise both political parties on a nonpartisan basis. In short, they felt that women would have a chance to make the world a better place if they worked within their own separate sphere.

As support for woman suffrage increased so did the rancor between the suffrage and antisuffrage women, each group unfathomable to and intolerant of the other. Women on both sides of the issue accused their opponents of not being "real" women. Suffragists ridiculed antisuffragists as "useless parasites" and "a disgrace to their sex." The antisuffragists, horrified at militant suffragists picketing outside the White House while the country was at war, declared that woman suffrage would "be an endorsement of nagging as a national policy." Naturally each camp claimed to represent the majority of women.

Ironically the antisuffragists' effort to stay out of politics effectively politicized them, which helped reconcile them to woman suffrage when it finally passed. After all, once you have learned to debate, make speeches, lobby, campaign, fundraise, and organize on an issue, voting every two years doesn't seem so earth-shattering.

Today, while it would be easy enough to find a woman who did not vote in the last election, it would be difficult to find one who thought she should not have the right to vote. New issues have come to the forefront of the political debate, but they are just as hotly contested among women as suffrage was earlier. The history of women's political activism includes both the Phyllis Schlaflys and the Gloria Steinems. As far as I can tell, just about the only thing that the majority of women seemed to believe in during the era of the woman suffrage movement was that women are superior to men. I don't know if *that* belief has changed all that much.

THE STEREOTYPES ABOUT WOMEN CAN WORK TO THEIR ADVANTAGE

"A woman's place is in the home, taking care of her husband and family." This well-accepted sentiment was used repeatedly to justify excluding women from the political process. It was a pretty hard sentiment to refute because, for the most part, both women and men agreed with this definition of a woman's role.

(Indeed, the notion of equal rights was not terribly popular with the general audience; as one woman put it, "Why should I lower myself to be the equal of man?") Nevertheless, when women felt compelled to participate in the important debates of their day on such issues as slavery, temperance, social reform, and suffrage, many used the very argument of women's traditional role to explain their involvement.

When Northern women first started mass petitioning of Congress against slavery in the late 1830s, they acknowledged the controversy of their actions by admitting that politics was not the sphere to which a "divine and wise" providence had assigned them. But how, they argued, could they as mothers and wives stand by quietly when slave mothers were being torn from their children and when "the sacred domestic ties" were being rent asunder?

Frances Willard of the Woman's Christian Temperance Union recruited many conservative women to her activist agenda with the motto "To make the world more home-like" and the idea that the nation needed "the home protection ballot." The women involved in the settlement house movement and Progressive Era reforms used similar arguments with great effectiveness.

The increase in women entering administrative professions was explained by the idea of "public motherhood." In her 1910 book *What Eight Million Women Want,* suffragist Rheta Childe Dorr wrote: "Woman's place is in the home. This is a platitude which no woman will ever dissent from. . . . But Home is not contained within the four walls of an individual home. Home is the community. The city full of people is the Family. The public school is the real Nursery. And badly do the Home and the Family and the Nursery need their mother."

The Children's Bureau, the first federal agency to be headed by a woman (Julia Lathrop) and the first to devote itself to the cause of children, was created and funded by the lobbying persistence of women. Identifying themselves as the mothers of America, they organized a huge petition drive to Congress, arguing that surely the children of America were worthy of the same kinds of expenditure appropriated for "the raising of cabbages and the development of big hogs." What senator wanted the stigma of voting against the millions of mothers of America?

One of my favorite examples of using domestic stereotypes to women's advantage is a simple little pamphlet called *The Non Sense of It*. A piece of prosuffrage propaganda, it was circulated by women's rights activists after the Civil War in an attempt to enfranchise women along with the freedmen. (We found it in a box at the National Archives along with an 1866 "Universal Suffrage" petition to Congress signed by Elizabeth Cady Stanton, Susan B. Anthony, Lucy Stone, and many of the other great leaders of the suffrage movement.) It lists eight of the standard arguments used at the time against women voting. Underneath each argument is a sensible, humorous rebuke. Here are some examples:

The polls are not decent places for women at present.

Then she is certainly needed there to make them decent. Literature was not decent, nor the dinner table, till she was admitted to them, on equal terms. But already, throughout most parts of the country, the ballot-box is as quiet a place to go to as the Post-office; and where it is not so, the presence of one woman would be worth a dozen policemen.

Politics are necessarily corrupting.

Then why not advise good men, as well as good women, to quit voting?

A woman who takes proper care of her household, has no time to know anything about politics.

Why not say a man who properly supports his household, has no time to know anything about politics? Show me the husband who does not assure his wife that his day's work is harder than her's. How absurd, then, to suppose that he has time to read the newspaper every day, and step round to the ballot box once a year—and she has not?

Women, after all, are silly creatures.

No doubt they are, often enough. As the old lady says in a late English novel, "God Almighty made some of them foolish, to match the men." And the men have done their best to turn the heads of others, who were no fools by nature. But it is the theory of democracy that every man has a right to express his own folly at the ballot-box, if he will—and in time, perhaps, learn more sense by so doing. And why not every woman too?

What I like so much about *The Non Sense of It* is how easily it can be understood by the modern reader. What's more, it is funny—intentionally so—the sort of thing that David Letterman had he been around a century ago might have read on his show. Who would have thought that those early suffragists, with their high-necked dresses, pince-nez, and severe hairdos, could be so warm, so human, so very like women today?

In more modern times, women political candidates have capitalized with great success on stereotypes of women as more honest than men, specialists at making small budgets stretch, and better at representing the interests of women, children, and families. Women candidates are often viewed as being especially strong in a political climate exhausted by scandal—more than one candidate has played in her campaign upon the image of the woman sweeping a house clean with a broom.

The trick seems to be to see gender not as an obstacle to overcome but as an asset to be trumpeted. Barbara Sigmund, the late mayor of Princeton and one of my role models, used to say that she didn't know how anybody could ever be a mayor without first being a mother: "Everybody hanging on your skirts saying 'gimme this, gimme that'—they're just like children!"

THERE IS A LOT MORE TO DEMOCRACY THAN VOTING

The first election after women gained the right to vote was no big deal. I don't mean to imply that it wasn't enormously important to those women who had helped make suffrage a reality. It was just that, for the most part, things went on as normal. Women had the vote, but they didn't seem to vote all that differently from men. If the antisuffragists' dire predictions about soaring divorce rates didn't come true, neither did the suffragists' dreams of a utopian society. After a few years passed, people couldn't seem to remember what the fuss was all about. Why didn't something more noteworthy happen?

Part of the reason no marked change occurred is that although suffrage was official recognition of women's political participation, women had been influencing and making changes in American democracy all along. Long before the 19th Amendment was ratified, the 1st Amendment had given women the right to freedom of speech and of the press, the right to peaceably assemble, and the right to petition the government for a redress of grievances. So women debated and spoke in public, testified before congressional committees, and addressed state legislatures. In the early days of the suffrage movement, when no woman was allowed to stay in the "better" hotels unaccompanied by a man, Susan B. Anthony traveled all over the country and scandalized people by speaking to audiences of both men and women.

Later on, when the ranks of women working for suffrage swelled and public speaking for women became more acceptable, suffragists learned to drive their motorcars up to street corners and talk into empty space until a crowd formed. They were taught how to defuse hecklers and win the crowds to their cause with humor. As suffragist Maud Malone was speaking to a New York City crowd, a hostile male voice from the crowd interrupted her. "How'd you like to be a man?" the heckler sneered. "Not much," she replied. "How would you?"

Women became adept at grassroots organization. The staid traditional and hierarchical National American Woman Suffrage Association believed that the way to win the vote was by careful persuasion, lobbying, and the building up of relationships—a slow but inevitable process by which it helped make woman suffrage acceptable to the general public. Schools were set up for suffragists where they learned how to canvass their neighborhoods, set up suffrage clubs, and lobby local politicians.

Women's organizations such as the General Federation of Women's Clubs and the National Congress of Mothers formed special committees to track the political activities of their local, state, and national representatives. These committees interviewed prospective political candidates about their positions on issues and placed women in the galleries in capitols around the country to take careful notice of how their legislators voted.

Women wrote letters to their congressmen and editors, published columns in national newspapers, and made their living as professional reporters. When that wasn't enough, they published their own newspapers and other informational materials, complete with facts and statistics compiled through their own research.

The roles that women could play within government were changing as well. In the late 1800s, they made job inroads as civil servants, inspectors, judges, clerks, and public administrators. As lawyers, they argued cases in front of the Supreme Court, where they were admitted to practice in 1879.

Long before they could vote nationwide, women ran for the presidency of the United States (most notably Victoria Woodhull in 1872 and Belva Lockwood in 1884). They served as mayors, city councilwomen, school board representatives, and members of state legislatures. The voters of Oskaloosa, Kansas, elected the first all-female city government in 1888, as a protest against the mismanagement of the previous city council. The new city council enforced the laws, made several civic improvements, and brought the treasury from a debt to a surplus. The women were reelected the following year.

As not the least of these activities, in a time before CNN and public opinion polls, women collected tens of millions of signatures for hundreds of thousands of petitions supporting the legislation they believed in. In 1917, New York women collected over a million signatures on a petition to the state legislature from women seeking suffrage. To forestall accusations that they had inflated the number of signatures, the women put all the signature sheets on placards and marched, two and four abreast, in a procession that covered over half a mile. In the course of such ever growing political activity, women managed slowly to change the standards that dictated what women were allowed to do.

Although Susan B. Anthony did not live to see ratification of the amendment that was named for her, she was aware of the changes she and others had accomplished in their lifetimes, and she felt confident that women eventually would carry the day. This letter from Anthony to her great friend Elizabeth Cady Stanton, written days before Stanton's death in 1902, is reprinted in *The History of Woman Suffrage*.

> We little dreamed when we began this contest, optimistic with the hope and buoyancy of youth, that half a century later we would be compelled to leave the finish of the battle to another generation of women. But our hearts are filled with joy to know that they enter upon this task equipped with a college education, with business experience, with the fully admitted right to speak in public—all of which were denied to women fifty years ago. They have practically but one point to gain—the suffrage: we had all. These strong, courageous, capable young women will take our place and complete our work. There is an army of them where we were but a handful. Ancient prejudice has become so softened, public sentiment so liberalized and women have so thoroughly demonstrated their ability to leave not a shadow of doubt that they will carry our cause to victory.

As odd as it may sound, one of the most important lessons of the woman suffrage movement may be the relative unimportance of suffrage all by itself. Around election time, television commentators talk about how few eligible voters actually vote. Celebrities and nonprofit groups produce eye-catching public service announcements to convince us to participate in this most minimal requirement of democracy. But voting is something we do at most once a year, and by itself, it is not always the best way to communicate with Washington.

The messages we voters send can be very confusing. Politicians cannot read our minds, and polling is a notoriously unreliable way of ascertaining just how strongly people care about an issue. Technically we are a republic, not a democracy. When we vote, we authorize someone else to make myriad decisions for us so that we don't have to spend all our own time thinking about the gross domestic product and dairy regulation and U.S. political interests in Burkina Faso. But many rights other than the vote are guaranteed by the Constitution, rights that we are able to—and need to—take advantage of if we want to influence our government more directly. Democracy requires a lot of day-to-day maintenance; going to school board meetings is much more effective than just complaining about the educational system.

The struggle for woman suffrage is traditionally believed to have started in 1848, when the right to vote was included among the resolutions passed at the Seneca Falls women's rights convention. Only one of the original signers at the convention, a young glove maker named Charlotte Woodward, would live to see the 19th Amendment ratified seventy-two years later. It is not surprising that one of the constant frustrations of suffrage organizers was how long the struggle was taking. But perhaps the long wait was not such a terrible thing. The years of hard work women put into making suffrage a reality taught them the full potential of democracy and how to employ that potential. They learned grassroots skills and gained the political credentials that made them more effective and laid the groundwork for their increasing participation in government. After all, the vote alone should never be the goal; the goal is what you can do with the vote.

I end with the words of Helen Keller in her article "Why Men Need Woman Suffrage," published in 1915 by the *New York Call* newspaper. "Women insist on their 'divine rights,' 'immutable rights,' 'inalienable rights.' These phrases are not so sensible as one might wish. When one comes to think of it, there are no such things as divine, immutable or inalienable rights. Rights are things which we get when we are strong enough to make good our claim to them. Men spent hundreds of years and much hard fighting to get the rights they now call divine, immutable and inalienable. Today women are demanding rights that tomorrow nobody will be foolish enough to question."

ELISABETH GRIFFITH is a historian, educator, and author. She is headmistress of the Madeira School, an independent school for girls in grades 9 to 12. The author of *In Her Own Right* (1984), a biography of Elizabeth Cady Stanton, she is currently writing a history of the Equal Rights Amendment. A former fellow of the Institute of Politics at Harvard's Kennedy School of Government, Griffith has taught history at the American University and the National Cathedral School. She is a board member of the Association of Independent Schools of Greater Washington and the National Association of Principals of Schools for Girls and the former chair of the Women's Campaign Fund. A graduate of Wellesley College, she earned an M.A. degree from Johns Hopkins University and a Ph.D. degree in history from the American University.

The Politics of Sisterhood

ELISABETH GRIFFITH

F OR MORE THAN TWO HUNDRED YEARS, Fourth of July fireworks, parades, and band concerts have marked the birth of American democracy in 1776. Yet celebratory sentiments have not always been unanimous. Those citizens whose rights had been ignored by the Founding Fathers at the signing of the Declaration of Independence had reasons to protest.

On July 4, 1854, abolitionist William Lloyd Garrison burned a copy of the Constitution to demonstrate his disillusionment with a nation, supposedly founded on the ideals of justice and liberty, that enslaved four million blacks. The crowd of 3,000 affirmed his protest with a tremendous "Amen!" Henry David Thoreau joined Garrison at the Framingham, Massachusetts, rally, declaring, "my thoughts are murder to the State." That same year he issued his personal declaration of independence by publishing *Walden,* which recalled his move on

July 4 some years earlier to an isolated cabin in the woods to protest a corrupt and violent society.

On July 4, 1855, Walt Whitman published *Leaves of Grass,* in defiance of the "swarms of cringers, suckers, doughfaces, lice of politics," who infested government (*New York Times,* July 4, 1995). Such gestures contributed to a tradition of revolutionary patriotic protest by white men that stretches from Tom Paine to Tom Hayden.

But those same liberal men blanched when confronted by proof of their own discrimination. On July 4, 1858, abolitionist agent Henry Brewster Stanton celebrated the holiday by taking five of his six children on a picnic. His wife stayed home with the baby and considered declaring domestic independence. This letter from Elizabeth Cady Stanton to her lieutenant, Susan B. Anthony, appears in my biography of Stanton, *In Her Own Right.*

> Oh how I long for a few hours of blessed leisure each day. How rebellious it makes me feel when I see Henry going about where and how he pleases. He can walk at will through the whole wide world or shut himself up alone. . . . As I contrast his freedom with my bondage, and feel that, because of the false position of women, I have been compelled to hold all my noblest aspirations in abeyance in order to be a wife, a mother, a nurse, a cook, a household drudge, I am fired anew and long to pour forth from my own experience the whole long story of women's wrongs. I have been alone today as the whole family except Hattie and myself have been out to celebrate our national birthday. What has woman to do with patriotism? Must not someone watch baby, house and garden?

Even the most enlightened men resisted change. John Adams, as we all know, ignored his wise wife's warning. "[R]emember the ladies," wrote Abigail Smith Adams to her delegate husband on March 31, 1776, "and be more generous and favorable to them than your ancestors. Do not put such unlimited power into the hands of the husbands. Remember, all men would be tyrants if they could. If particular care and attention is not paid to the ladies, we are determined to foment a rebellion, and will not hold ourselves bound by any laws in which we have no voice, or representation."

Abigail Adams recognized that the Declaration of Independence and later the Constitution were not democratic but discriminatory documents. Blacks, whether freemen or slaves, were not the only Americans excluded. Women who had voted in the Colonies as white property owners twenty-one or older (meaning women without fathers, brothers, husbands, or sons to control their assets) lost that right when state constitutions defined citizenship by gender. Only New Jersey failed to disenfranchise women, until 1807. Pioneer women would win back this right because on the frontier they were valued as equal economic partners. In 1869, the territory of Wyoming allowed women to vote; it entered the Union in 1890 as the first full suffrage state. Before 1920 and ratification of the 19th Amendment, women voted in fifteen states; all except Michigan and New York were west of the Mississippi. Montana elected Jeannette Rankin as the first woman member of Congress in 1916.

But not until Elizabeth Cady Stanton and Lucretia Coffin Mott launched the first American women's rights movement in 1848 did anyone even question citizenship based on gender. In mid July of that year, Stanton, Mott, and three other women hosted the first women's rights convention in America, in Seneca Falls, New York.

Stanton shocked even her staunchest friends by demanding voting rights for women, along with seventeen other platform planks urging property rights, educational opportunities, and economic equity. "Thee will make us appear ridiculous," worried Stanton's mentor, Mrs. Mott, a Quaker abolitionist whose husband James chaired the meeting on the first day because any woman speaking to a "mixed" male and female audience in those days was condemned as "promiscuous." On the second day, however, he invited his wife to the podium and sat in the front row holding her bonnet.

These Founding Mothers issued the Declaration of Sentiments, which paraphrased the Declaration of Independence but addressed "all

men" as the oppressor, instead of "the present King of Great Britain."
Every resolution except woman suffrage passed unanimously. Only
after Frederick Douglass, who had escaped slavery and then edited *The
North Star* newspaper in Rochester, New York, allied himself with
Stanton's cause did the controversial plank pass, narrowly. Sixty-eight
women and thirty-two men signed the final document. Such audacity
might have been overlooked had an Associated Press telegraph line not
recently linked Seneca Falls to the rest of the country. Newspaper editors and ministers thundered their disapproval.

It would be seventy-two years before woman suffrage succeeded.
"Young suffragists who helped forge the last links of that chain were
not born when it began; old suffragists who helped forge the first links
were dead when it ended," Carrie Chapman Catt summarized in 1920.
Stanton's political if not philosophical successor as president of the National American Woman Suffrage Association (NAWSA) and founder
of the League of Women Voters (LWV), Catt enumerated the efforts required to win the vote after victory in 1920: "56 referenda to male voters; 480 efforts to get state legislatures to submit suffrage amendments;
277 campaigns to get state party conventions to include women's suffrage planks; 47 campaigns to get state constitutional conventions to
write women's suffrage into state constitutions; 30 campaigns to get
presidential party conventions to adopt women's suffrage planks
in party platforms; and 19 successive campaigns with 19 successive
Congresses."

Catt failed to mention the cost: the enormous amounts of money
raised to fund each successive campaign; the individual sacrifices of
women whose names have not been recorded; the exacerbated tensions
between black and white women and men, who had earlier been allies;
and the animosity among suffrage leaders, which would poison their
success and linger like the bad fairy's curse to metastasize during the
campaign to ratify the Equal Rights Amendment.

Finally, in 1918, the suffrage amendment passed in the House of
Representatives by exactly the two-thirds majority necessary, but it was
then defeated in the Senate. In four states where women had already

won the vote, NAWSA organized campaigns to defeat senators who had voted against the amendment. Two of these campaigns were successful; two were enough of a threat to turn the tide. In June of the following year, the Senate finally passed the suffrage amendment and sent it to the states for ratification. Several states rushed to ratify, but stiff opposition gripped the Northeast and South. After fourteen months of lobbying, letter writing, and petitioning, the 19th Amendment passed (as Eleanor Flexner reports in *Century of Struggle*) due to the single vote of Harry Burn, a twenty-four-year-old Tennessee state legislator, on the orders of his mother, a steadfast suffragist: "Don't forget to be a good boy and help Mrs. Catt."

Winning suffrage deserved fireworks and cheering in the streets. Instead, the participants snubbed each other. When the amendment was to be signed, on August 26, 1920, both President Wilson and Vice President Thomas R. Marshall refused to attend. Moreover, by this time, there were two distinct factions in the suffragist movement, and the leaders did not want to share credit at the signing. Secretary of State Bainbridge Colby decided to sign the proclamation at home, "to avoid a clash at his office," said the *New York Times*. He signed the document at 8:00 A.M. with no suffrage leaders present, and he refused to restage the event for cameras.

Who deserved credit for the success of woman suffrage is still hotly debated by historians and by the partisans of Catt on the one hand and of Alice Paul, head of the National Woman's Party (NWP), on the other. Paul represented the third generation of suffragists in this mother-daughter-granddaughter struggle. A feisty Quaker pacifist who imported the outdoor protest tactics of British suffragists, she organized 5,000 women wearing white to march down Pennsylvania Avenue the day President-elect Woodrow Wilson arrived at Union Station for his March 1913 inauguration. Paul and NWP members picketed the White House; when arrested, they launched a prison hunger strike. Never convinced that suffrage alone was enough, in 1923, Paul proposed the Equal Rights Amendment, returning to Seneca Falls on the 75th anniversary of that first women's rights convention.

To Carrie Chapman Catt, recruited to the suffrage cause by Susan B. Anthony, Alice Paul was a troublemaker whose tactics disrupted Catt's carefully constructed "Winning Plan." The animosity between Paul and Catt, between the NWP and NAWSA (later the LWV), was intimate and intense. I believe its legacy undermined the success of the second women's rights movement launched in the 1960s, whose centerpiece was another effort to pass the Equal Rights Amendment, even though only Paul was still alive to remember.

Because the League of Women Voters and the majority of postsuffrage activists believed that women needed protective labor legislation regulating hours and conditions of work rather than equal status, and because Catt detested Paul and Paul never forgot Catt's condemnation, the LWV steadfastly opposed the Equal Rights Amendment for many years. Not until 1972, did the LWV publicly change its position, and then some longstanding ERA advocates, like the Business and Professional Women (BPW), supporters since 1937, initially resented rather than welcomed the LWV action.

Reflecting back on those heroic woman suffragists and the heady days of their struggle, I am filled with admiration for their fortitude and with frustration over their inability to work together. The suffrage campaign required both political savvy and passionate protest. For Catt and Paul and their successors, the political became too personal. We need to remember not only the lessons we have learned about the remarkable success of essentially powerless women dependent on male politicians, but also the lessons we have forgotten about the vulnerability of coalitions and the politics of sisterhood.

There are many ironies. The ERA coalition, incapable of long-term cohesion, attempted to combat Phyllis Schlafly, head of Stop ERA, whose skills as an organizer and demagogue were reminiscent of Catt's and Paul's skills combined. Her anti-ERA rhetoric echoed the sentiments made generations earlier by antisuffragists. Schlafly's single ladylike voice silenced the strident cries of the National Organization for Women (NOW), the reasoned arguments of the LWV, the historical perspective of the BPW, and the vast majority of nurses, teachers, mothers, nuns, labor union workers, blacks and Hispanics, and men and women in poll after poll.

The coalition suffered from rivalry among allies competing for air-time and credit. To its discredit, it allowed the media to define the question and divide its ranks: homemakers versus working women, blacks versus whites, gays versus straights, pro-life versus pro-choice. In the end, the LWV once again provided cool-headed, effective strategies; the BPW provided large portions of the budget and, along with other organizations, a grassroots network. NOW played the part once played by the NWP, grandstanding, boycotting, protesting. We were unable to find a way to combine our talents to strengthen the whole.

Until the current women's movement can set aside its organizational rivalries and internecine hairsplitting to focus on the unfinished agenda (Stanton's 1848 Declaration of Sentiments might suffice), it will continue to flounder. Catt and Paul are dead. There have been no worthy successors. We need to seek out leaders who have learned from the legacy and lessons of our shared past.

SARAH McCLENDON has been a news reporter since 1931. She is
founder and owner of McClendon News Service in Washington,
D.C., publishing a bimonthly newsletter and a syndicated column
and broadcasting daily on two radio networks. A native of Tyler,
Texas, she served in World War II as a public affairs officer in the
Women's Army Auxiliary Corps. She is a past vice president of
the National Press Club, to which she was admitted only after
twenty-seven years of being qualified but female. She helped open
Veterans of Foreign Wars to eligible women veterans and opened
the Texas congressional delegation luncheons and the Texas
Breakfast Club to women. She is a former president of the
American Newspaper Women's Club, a commander in American
Legion Post #20, and a member and adviser to the board of the
National Woman's Party.

The Women's Movement Across Generations

SARAH McCLENDON

MORE THAN SEVENTY-FIVE YEARS have passed since women at-
tained the right to vote, and although women today are 53 percent of the population and vote in larger numbers than men, women
still are not treated as equals.

While women have made great strides in the United States and the
world, women still are not equal under the law; in the workplace; in
government and private-sector benefits; in receiving health protection
and research on their health; in their treatment by the banking, real es-
tate, and insurance industries; in institutions of learning; or in the arts.
We have had some breakthroughs, however. Certainly more recognition is now given to women and their presence in the body politic and
in civic affairs than ever before. But still women are not equal in the
rights and privileges afforded by American citizenship.

American women seem to make gains and then experience a back-lash and setbacks. Now, a definite forced retreat for women appears to be under way. Conservatives in Congress are steadily rewriting laws to erode protections for women. They blame women for part of the nation's deficit because of vast sums spent on welfare. They charge openly that some women are purposely getting pregnant because if they have more babies they get higher monthly government payments.

Before the American Revolution, some unmarried white women were permitted to vote because they owned property. After the Revolution, as states began to write constitutions that included the qualifications for suffrage, women lost the vote. New Jersey was an exception; it kept ownership of property as the criterion for voting until 1807, when it passed a new electoral law specifically excluding women. The first state to permit women to vote once again was Kentucky, which in 1838 allowed widows to vote for school board members. Then, in 1859, Kansas extended school board suffrage to all women. Finally, in 1869, the territory of Wyoming granted full suffrage to women.

THE WOMAN SUFFRAGE MOVEMENT

I thank God I was born into the movement for woman suffrage. My mother, Mrs. S. S. McClendon, was a suffragist and, having no baby-sitter at the time, she took me with her when she went out with the late Mrs. Johnson into surrounding East Texas towns to speak to women's groups to get votes for woman suffrage. This must have been 1916, when I was a child of six, and I noted then that when I came home and pantomimed the speakers, my elder brothers made fun of woman suffrage. Why did they and many young men resist the idea of women voting?

Years later, I saw freshmen at the U.S. Naval Academy bitterly re-sentful that women were to be allowed to enter the academy for the first time. How could these young men hold this attitude when they had not yet even seen the women or watched them in classes? When Shannon Faulkner, the Citadel's first woman student, dropped out of that military academy in 1995, the male cadets danced with glee. Why? Were they born with this bias against women? If it did not come from home, how did it happen? We must teach the women who give birth to these men and rear them how to instill in their sons a different attitude toward women.

The struggles of the suffragists carry some lessons for us about persistence and the importance of instilling new views in others if we are to further women's rights. The movement for woman suffrage officially began in 1848, when the first women's rights conference was held. Much later, in 1913, Alice Paul of New Jersey came to Washington and organized the Congressional Union, later the National Woman's Party. The right to vote was one of her main objectives. Another was the Equal Rights Amendment to the Constitution. It was only after many attempts and many disappointments that Alice Paul and women leaders in several other organizations were able to get Congress to send the women's voting rights amendment on its way to passage in 1919 and ratification in 1920. This victory was indeed sweet. Women who choose not to vote today relinquish their part in democracy.

The right to vote was won with the help of President Woodrow Wilson, who refused even to look at the woman suffrage demonstrators at first but became an immense help in the end. The struggle to win the vote was undertaken by both militant and moderate groups of women, and it was the moderate National American Woman Suffrage Association (NAWSA), led by Anna Howard Shaw and Carrie Chapman Catt, that worked with President Wilson.

While the militants under Alice Paul opened the doors to acceptance of the idea of woman suffrage, many observers think that the more moderate NAWSA brought about congressional acceptance. However, Hazel Hunkins Hallinan, working with Alice Paul, certainly helped get the president's attention by climbing over the fence in front of the White House and setting a fire on the grounds. Hallinan related this story to me as we marched side by side in a Women's Equality Day parade in Washington, D.C., with the National Woman's Party and other organizations more than half a century later. Hallinan and Paul suffered for their cause. They fought for woman suffrage in England and the United States. Paul was imprisoned in both countries; she went on hunger strikes and was force-fed for her beliefs. Both women suffered the rigors of the Lorton, Virginia, prison and its rodents, bugs, and cold floors. A plaque memorializing their ordeal was placed on the wall of the National Woman's Party headquarters under the presidency of Alice Paul's successor, Elizabeth Chittick.

I knew Alice Paul. It was my pleasure once to have her speak to one of my study group sessions for women reporters at the Capitol. Paul could be uncompromising in her determination. She did not negotiate away her objectives. Not only did she lead the fight to get women the right to vote through a constitutional amendment, she also wrote the ERA, carefully drafting it to keep out extraneous controversial matters. Since the days of Alice Paul and the militant suffragists, the women's movement has lacked dynamic leadership concentrated on one goal such as the ERA.

WHY WE NEED THE ERA

Modern feminist legal and legislative advocacy to achieve equality under the law began in the early 1960s and flourished in the 1970s. Several important laws were enacted in the 1960s, mainly efforts to equalize women's economic and employment security. In 1963, after eighteen years of battle, the Equal Pay Act was passed, prohibiting unequal pay for equal or substantially equal work. This legislation came in a period when employers often advertised separately for male and female employees and females earned sixty cents for every dollar men earned.

Title VII of the Civil Rights Act of 1964, prohibiting employment discrimination, may be the most important protection women have in the workplace. Its passage was not without irony, however. On the assumption that the inclusion of women would kill the Civil Rights bill, an ardent segregationist amended Title VII to include sex discrimination. Fortunately his strategy backfired on him.

Women are often still excluded from opportunities related to work. It took me twenty-seven years to become a member of the National Press Club, although I was a qualified journalist all that time and worked in the Press Club building. When I finally was permitted to attend the Press Club's Christmas party for children, I took my daughter and my granddaughter! In order to have an office in that important building, I was forced to share one with a club member, a man. When a head of state came to speak, I had to sit or stand upstairs in the auditorium balcony to listen. No food was provided. I could not ask a question. When I was elected club vice president, the club leaders said it was an accident and changed the rules for electing officers.

I took the issue up with President John Kennedy at a press conference—what did he think of his own cabinet heads speaking at the Press Club when women reporters could not be members? He had not known of the discrimination but expressed his disagreement with the club's policy. Of course, he was an honorary member. When the heads of state of India and the USSR came to Washington, they declared they would not speak at the Press Club unless women were allowed admittance. Finally women were admitted, largely due to the efforts of a former club president, Don Larrahee. I was one of the first women members. My application, duly signed by male members, had lain dormant for years.

In the 1970s, the U.S. Supreme Court heard a number of cases involving sex discrimination that challenged the equal protection guarantees of the 14th Amendment and the due process clause of the 5th Amendment. However, the Supreme Court has never interpreted the protections of the Constitution as applying to sex discrimination in the same manner as it uses in cases of racial or ethnic discrimination. The Court came close in the 1973 case of *Frontiero* v. *Richardson*, when Justices William Brennan, Thurgood Marshall, Byron White, and William Douglas agreed that sex discrimination should receive the Court's "strict scrutiny." Writing for this four-member plurality, Justice

Brennan described the history of sex discrimination in the United States as "'romantic paternalism,' which, in practical effect, put women, not on a pedestal, but in a cage." But no other Justice provided the fifth vote needed to achieve a majority. Rather than join the plurality, Justice Lewis Powell argued that since the ERA had gone to the states for ratification, the Court should not interfere with the democratic process.

It is history of this kind that tells us of our absolute need for inclusion of women in the Constitution through adoption of the Equal Rights Amendment. Even though the ERA was introduced in every Congress since Alice Paul first proposed it in 1923, Congress did not pass it until 1972. Eventually thirty-five states ratified it, but thirty-eight are needed to amend the Constitution. Some women who opposed the ERA were intimidated by fundamentalist preachers in the South who told them that supporting it was an act of disobedience to their religious principles. Of course there was no sin in supporting ERA, but this and similar misrepresentations had their day. Although the ERA ratification effort begun in 1972 died in 1982, the amendment is always reintroduced in each new Congress.

Currently two strategies have been proposed to ratify the ERA. One would bypass the mandate that this amendment had to be ratified in a certain time period. Other amendments to the Constitution have not had a time limit on their ratification. For example, the Madison Amendment was declared ratified in 1992 by adding up all the states that had approved it since 1789. The other strategy would revive the ERA if any three new states ratify it; this proposal would relieve proponents from having to seek reratification from the thirty-five states that approved ERA in the 1970s and 1980s.

SEXUAL HARASSMENT

Sexual harassment is sex discrimination. Why do men harass women? It does not make any sense. Once the Navy analyzed an admiral's persistent harassment of the women serving under him. They concluded his behavior was due in part to his belief that the women were his inferiors. Apparently the instinct to exercise power over a "lesser" crea-ture enters into many cases of sexual harassment. Compounding the problem is the lack of penalties handed out to offenders. When I served on the Defense Advisory Committee on Women in the Services and committee members assessed such cases, I noted that the worst penalty the Marine Corps thought it could issue for them was to put a man out of the corps. There was no attempt to go through a court-martial.

In talking to a number of young women in the military recently, I learned that the situation is much worse now than when I was in the service in World War II. I was told of superior officers laying out two papers on their desks at promotion time; one paper is the promotion and one is not. These officers invite the young women to go to bed with them and then inquire which paper the women want? In disgust, but frightened, some young women have given into this worst form of intimidation.

Five women employees of the Veterans Administration in Massa-chusetts, New Jersey, and California decided they would do something to stop such harassment. They appealed to the House of Repre-sentatives Committee on Veterans Affairs, which gave them a public hearing. These women made a difference. They told how employment policies permitted harassers to be transferred—not fired, not punished, simply put in another office where they often continued their miscon-duct. A woman who reports sexual harassment is often not believed. Her case may drag on for many months or years. She is devastated. She may have to have psychiatric care, which the government does not pay for. She finds it horrifying to run into the same man again at work. She may be in such a devastated state that she cannot work. She may be fired. She experiences the distrust of her superiors and others. The of-fender may simply be transferred to another job in another office; he continues to get his pay check and is secure in his job.

What happened after these five brave women sought to reform a whole system? Their action prompted more reporting of incidents and stirred up a delayed public conscience. One woman who testified about her experiences started a newsletter, entitled WASH (Women Against

Sexual Harassment), which now is distributed among women in government service. The hearings resulted in legislation that would strengthen the procedures when an individual files a claim of sexual harassment. It passed the House in 1994 but died in the Senate. Although sexual harassment is a crucial problem and is governmentwide, very little is being done to give women relief. This is but another example of how women are not given full citizenship.

Sexual harassment does not occur only in the Department of Veterans Affairs, although more reports have been filed there than in other departments. In a case at the Internal Revenue Service, one young woman, a new employee, was invited to a company party. When she arrived, she found she was the only woman. Later she learned she was to be the entertainment for the evening. She encountered all kinds of harassment for failing to comply with their schemes. She reported the case to superiors and endured lengthy inquisitions, all the time seeing no change or punishment for males involved. Then came long delays at the Equal Employment Opportunity office. Even a woman chief told her it would be at least a year before that office could take up the case. Others have reported long delays or no action by the government officers who are supposed to look into these cases and give some form of relief to the victims.

A woman who was abducted from in front of the officers' club at Andrews Air Base in Maryland reported her case to the police as soon as she was released. Later they told her they could find no record of her assault. She paid the price. She endured prolonged psychiatric treatment, was unable to work, was denied food stamps, became homeless, and lived for two years on the streets. Finally a woman veterans' counselor found the police report and helped this woman.

Sexual harassment is not limited to the military and government; it is much worse in the corporate world. Moreover, it is not always aimed at the young woman; it also can happen to older employees. Yet a lack of willingness to help women solve the problem of sexual harassment seems obvious among citizens in general as well as among members of Congress, executives in government and business, and the judiciary.

MOVING FORWARD

Fifty-five is a record number for women serving in Congress; it was reached after the 1992 election. These congresswomen are largely responsible for the passage of laws that have improved the lives of women and families. Working as a bipartisan team, the congresswomen in the 103rd Congress can be credited with several major victories:

The Family and Medical Leave Act of 1993. This boon to men as well as women passed after eight years and two presidential vetoes. It provides for unpaid leave of absence to male and female workers to care for a newborn or newly adopted child, a seriously ill child or parent, or their own illness.

The Women's Health Equity Act. As a result of this act, which was incorporated in the National Institutes of Health reauthorization passed in 1993, the nation now has an office of Women's Health Research at the National Institutes of Health and a law requiring that women, once routinely excluded, be included in medical research studies unless there is some compelling reason to conduct an all-male study. A federally funded study is unlikely ever again to exclude women as did the Baltimore Longitudinal Study of Aging during its first twenty years (the reason given was that there was no women's bathroom where periodic physical exams were given to the participants). After the lack of attention to women's health issues was made known in Congress and in the press, funding was increased for research on cancers of the breast and reproductive tract and on osteoporosis and menopause.

The Violence Against Women Act. This act was incorporated in the omnibus crime legislation of 1994 that authorized nearly $2 billion dollars over six years to strengthen law enforcement efforts and provide services to victims of both domestic violence and sexual assault.

Then, in 1995, the new majority in the 104th Congress abolished more than one hundred caucuses, including the Congressional Caucus on Women's Issues. A funny thing about the women's caucus is this: men were admitted to membership in recent times, and when the caucus ended, more men belonged than women. Women members of Congress feel the loss of the caucus keenly because it functioned as a research institute on women's plight and supplied facts to Congress, the national press, and Washington think tanks. Caucus members immediately formed a new group, Women's Policy, Inc., to monitor Congress daily and to publish a weekly newsletter and a quarterly magazine on issues affecting women. Women members of Congress have also formed a bipartisan informal group called, simply, Congresswomen, which will continue advocacy on family issues.

Lesley Primmer, the executive director of Women's Policy, told me in an interview, "the 104th Congress is certainly the most anti-women's-issue Congress that I have seen in my fifteen years on Capitol Hill." Those issues include abortion rights, family planning, child care, gender equity, education, and violence against women. Also on the list are social service programs that serve low-income families, most of which are headed by women, and many programs that serve seniors, including Medicare. Primmer points out that issues affecting women and children are for the most part not partisan issues, "or at least they should not be; and it seems clear to me that moderates and progressives of both parties are going to have to band together if we are to hold the ground that we have won over the past twenty-five years."

A sympathetic voice for women throughout the world was heard when James Gustave Speth, administrator of the United Nations Development Programme, set the stage for the Fourth World Conference on Women, held in 1995. In his speech to the delegates, Speth noted that some less developed nations are showing more concern with the rights of women than the United States does—several countries, such as Finland, have had more women in their parliaments than this country has ever had in Congress—and he pointed to a U.N. human development report that shows the world would be better off economically and socially if women were paid their due for work done so that they could live above the poverty line. In other words, the world would benefit by ceasing to exploit women.

To cure the problems women face, we need more women to back equality of rights and benefits for women. Some women say they do not want to hear the matter discussed; some are totally uninterested in working toward equality. Moreover, the term *feminist* seems to turn off many women and men. Some congressmen tell me they have no reason to vote for equal rights for women because they have not heard from women in their district.

How do we get more women educated to believe in the movement? One difficulty is that not enough publicity has been given to educating the public on women's needs. Women who work for the advancement of women are usually unfamiliar with public relations or how to handle the media. They need professional help, which, while it costs money, can make a great difference towards victory. Also, women leaders have a tendency to be shy and secretive. For example, the Council of Presidents, composed of leaders of various organizations of women with headquarters in Washington, keeps its deliberations secret from other women. A nationwide campaign to inform the public on the problems caused by the exclusion and mistreatment of women in the past and the dangers of losing women's gains in the present would help bring many more women into the movement for equality.

Women fought for generations to win the right to vote. Women now have power at the polls and make up the majority of the voting-age population. We can elect presidents and choose Congresses. We have a right and responsibility to make our voices heard on all of the important policy debates under way in the Congress and to vote for women and men who will take very seriously the things we believe are important, holding them accountable to act on our behalf.

SARA E. MELÉNDEZ is president of the Independent Sector, a nonprofit coalition of more than 800 corporate, foundation, and voluntary organizations. From 1991 to 1994, she was president of the Center for Applied Linguistics. She is former vice provost and acting dean of arts and humanities of the University of Bridgeport; a past director, special minority initiatives, at the American Council on Education; a former trustee of Monmouth College; and a past president of the National Association for Bilingual Education. A native of Puerto Rico, Meléndez is a graduate of Brooklyn College and earned an M.Ed. degree from Long Island University and an Ed.D. degree from the Harvard Graduate School of Education. She is a trustee of the Educational Testing Service and serves on the boards of Quality Education for Minorities, CIVICUS, and the National Puerto Rican Forum.

American Democracy: A Puerto Rican Perspective

SARA E. MELÉNDEZ

M Y MOTHER WAS BORN in Puerto Rico the year that woman suffrage finally passed in the United States Congress and that the League of Women Voters was conceived. Two years before, in 1917, the United States had granted citizenship to residents of the Island of Puerto Rico, an American possession since the end of the Spanish-American War. That citizenship is limited, however: Puerto Ricans living on the U.S. mainland have the same rights of citizenship as those born on the mainland, but those living in Puerto Rico have no voting representation in Congress and cannot vote in presidential elections.

While many justify this modified citizenship on the grounds that Puerto Ricans on the Island of Puerto Rico do not pay federal taxes, many others resent the power over the island exercised by a Congress in which Puerto Ricans have no vote. The issue of the status of Puerto Rico has been a major factor in the lives of Puerto Ricans everywhere. Are we Puerto Ricans or Americans or Puerto Rican Americans? The issue does not appear to be close to a permanent solution.

However, woman suffrage has made a tremendous impact on the lives of Puerto Rican women on both the mainland and the island. In Puerto Rico, woman suffrage was not passed until 1929, when women who were literate were given the privilege. Finally, in 1936, suffrage in Puerto Rico was made universal, regardless of one's ability to read.

Although Puerto Rico took longer than the mainland to enact suffrage for women, it has a long history of women's involvement in politics. The Taino Indians, the indigenous people of Puerto Rico, had women tribal chiefs. And a woman who was a political pioneer, even by United States standards, Feliza Rincón de Gautier, became mayor of San Juan in the 1940s. My mother, a cook, maid, and seamstress with a third-grade education, told me proudly about working for one of Mayor Rincón's campaigns. She would have been very proud today to see a Puerto Rican woman in Congress. Nydia Velázquez, elected in 1992, is the first Puerto Rican woman member of the U.S. House of Representatives; several other Latinas are also members of Congress.

Puerto Rican women share many issues with all other women: the lack of equal pay for equal work, of adequate health care, and of adequate child and elder care and the risk of physical and sexual abuse and sexual harassment. On the one hand, such problems are compounded and exacerbated by racism, discrimination, and poverty. Even though the quality of life for many Puerto Rican women and their children has improved, many are still playing catch-up. The right to vote is meaningless to women who cannot see any direct benefit to themselves from exercising that right. On the other hand, middle-class Puerto Rican women are often very involved politically. The National Conference of Puerto Rican Women, a national organization with chapters in ten cities, has made voter registration and electoral participation of Latino citizens its number one priority through the 1996 elections.

As a Puerto Rican woman, I always have been acutely interested in the right of suffrage. I felt disenfranchised when I spent a year living in Puerto Rico as an adult. To those of us born since American women became full citizens, the idea of not being allowed to participate in the electoral process is inconceivable. Equally inconceivable is the idea that the

United States did not welcome the participation of half of its population until two decades into the twentieth century. Moreover, I have no doubt that woman suffrage contributed to the changes over the past seventy-five years that have affected the quality of life for all women, including myself. My mother's life was so different from mine that had she lived to see that difference, she might not have been able to comprehend it.

She migrated to the mainland at the age of twenty-six, leaving her three young children in the care of their grandmother. For two years, she worked as a sewing machine operator in the garment industry of New York City to support her children in Puerto Rico and herself in New York and to save enough money to send for her children to join her.

My mother left her home and family because there was no work in Puerto Rico for a young woman with a third-grade education that would permit her to support her children and live with dignity. She was very proud of her independence and taught her children the values of getting an education, working hard, and being good contributing citizens. She died of cancer at the age of thirty-nine, missing my high school graduation by three months. While she dreamed of my going to college, it never occurred to her, nor to me, that I would one day have a doctorate from Harvard.

In one generation, my family demonstrated the possibilities that exist in a democracy that provides opportunities. However, my experience also demonstrates the waste of potential and talent that occurs when worthy individuals who start out at a disadvantage do not receive a helping hand. I had at least fifty female Puerto Rican classmates in my high school graduating class, yet I was the only one who went on to earn a college degree. Many of the others were very bright but needed a little support or assistance and did not receive it.

The civil rights movement and the women's movement, two good examples of the democratic process at work, have resulted in the opening up of many more opportunities and options for women as well as some support by way of scholarships, counseling, mentoring programs, women's studies programs, and the phenomenal growth in research that has validated women's experience and contributions. The expanded presence of women in Congress has increased attention paid to such issues as women's health, physical and sexual abuse and sexual harassment, and marital property rights. In the political arena, we still have much work to do, however. The group of women who are currently active is too small to allow for ideological diversity and for success on many important women's issues.

The most encouraging fact about the progress made since woman suffrage is that women's lives have changed so much. The most discouraging fact is that for too many women they have changed so little. Seventy-five years after passage of the 19th Amendment, women earn more than half the bachelor's degrees and about half of the master's degrees awarded in this country. We make up 46 percent of the labor force and are making inroads into corporate boardrooms, but 95 percent of top corporate management positions are still held by white men. However, there is hope for the future, given that women now hold 35 percent of the management positions.

Puerto Rican women also have gained entry to corporate offices but are virtually nowhere to be found in boardrooms; that should begin to change. During the decade of the 1980s, more than 300,000 Puerto Ricans migrated to the mainland. Unlike the members of the last mass migration of Puerto Ricans to the mainland in the 1950s, many of these new migrants hold college and professional degrees; more than half are women. Perhaps due to the influx of well-educated Puerto Ricans, median household income for mainland Puerto Ricans increased by 30 percent during the 1980s, the highest increase for any ethnic group.

But for many Puerto Rican women on the U.S. mainland, the picture remains bleak. They and their children are among the poorest of Americans, partly due to a high rate of female-headed households (43 percent). Not surprisingly these Puerto Rican women have a lower educational attainment than white and African American women. They smoke more than other groups of women and have one of the highest rates of AIDS and HIV and the highest rate of diabetes of any group in the United States. A May 1995 American Medical Association–Harris poll conducted on women's reproduction revealed that Latinas are less likely than Anglo or African American women to know about birth control options, access to abortion, and other health topics. They also are less likely to consult a health care professional regularly.

Puerto Rican women, along with all women and people of color, have benefited from programs designed to address poverty among women and children. When educational opportunities opened up, they flocked to higher education and significantly increased their attainment of degrees. They have been moving steadily into new fields of work and up the ranks. It is clear, however, that the American dream is still beyond reach for many.

Now we have entered into a new phase of American history in which people are questioning some fundamental assumptions about the social contract; the programs that improved the lot in life of so many women from all groups are threatened. Reductions in budget allocations to meet the basic human needs of housing, health care, and education suggest that the safety net to protect poor women and their children will be dismantled within the next few years.

The 75th anniversary of woman suffrage should be a time of celebration, but also a time of our rededication and commitment to improve the quality of life for so many women who have not yet achieved their potential. For Puerto Rican women, progress is tied inextricably to the issues of equity, justice, and opportunity for all Puerto Ricans.

A mystique surrounds the arrival of a new millennium. With a new century comes the opportunity to start afresh or to make new century resolutions. We women constitute over half the population, but we have not yet used our political power to our maximum advantage. Understandably women are not monolithic; we come in all political persuasions. But all of us, whatever our affiliations, must learn to affirm our rights and those of our sisters. Although our celebration of the 19th Amendment may be somewhat dampened by the country's apparent backtracking on issues we thought we already had won, we must work together across class, race, and ethnic lines to ensure that our daughters and granddaughters will be full citizens and partners in the America of the twenty-first millennium.

When MARTINA NAVRATILOVA retired from playing professional singles tennis on the women's circuit in 1994, she had won more overall titles than any other woman or man in tennis history, including a record 167 career singles titles and a Grand Slam total of 58: 18 singles, 31 doubles, and 7 mixed doubles. She continues her doubles career, is a three-time president of the WTA TOUR Players Association, and is active in the Women's Sports Foundation. She is an advocate for gay rights, organizations benefiting children, AIDS, the environment, animal welfare, and women's issues. In 1995 she won the mixed doubles title at Wimbledon, became a tennis analyst for CBS and HBO, and published the first of her "Jordan Myles" mystery novels; her second, *Breaking Point*, was published in 1996.

No More Sounds of Silence

MARTINA NAVRATILOVA

W HEN I DEFECTED to the United States in 1975, the country
was getting ready to celebrate its 200th birthday. There was
excitement everywhere, and the pride I felt knowing that I would soon
become an American citizen was overwhelming.

Just 199 years before, the authors of the Declaration of Independence had written: "We hold these truths to be self-evident, that all men
are created equal, that they are endowed by their Creator with certain
unalienable rights, that among these are life, liberty and the pursuit of
happiness." I would have liked them to include *women,* and still do,
but the principle sounded great to me. My intention was to become the
number one woman tennis player in the world and to gratefully and
humbly enjoy the inalienable rights that my new country's forefathers
had guaranteed for all of us.

As I traveled around the United States from tennis tournament to tennis tournament after America's "bicentennial fever" subsided, I was often puzzled that so many people took my new country's basic rights for granted. I had a happy life with friends and family in Czechoslovakia until the Communists took over in 1968. After that our lives changed drastically, and I swore to myself that I would never take any rights of citizenship for granted.

I looked forward to the day when I could take my test and then be sworn in as a United States citizen. I loved studying for the citizenship exam, and I became more and more excited as I learned more about the country. Right there in the 1st Amendment in the Bill of Rights, some wise and farsighted men had written: "Congress shall make no law respecting an establishment of religion, or prohibiting the free exercise thereof; or abridging the freedom of speech, or of the press; or the right of the people peaceably to assemble . . ."

I was surprised when I found that it took until 1868 for the 14th Amendment to the Constitution to be ratified, since its language seemed to be the cornerstone of life in America. Nevertheless, reading, "No State shall make or enforce any law which shall abridge the privileges or immunities of citizens of the United States; . . . nor deny to any person within its jurisdiction the equal protection of the laws," guaranteed for me that what had happened to me in Czechoslovakia could never happen here.

But as soon as I became eligible to become a United States citizen in 1980, some harsh realities started to set in. I found I could not take the oath of citizenship in either Texas or Virginia, the two states where I had spent most of my time. I lived by the laws of the land and the Constitution. I paid my taxes. I had won a number of tennis tournaments, including four Wimbledon singles and doubles titles, three U.S. Open doubles crowns, and other Grand Slam tournaments, had been named Player of the Year by the Women's Tennis Association, and was currently serving as president of the Women's Tennis Association. Yet, in Virginia and Texas (and several other states), I could not apply for citizenship because, as a lesbian, I was considered a "law breaker."

I was a touring professional for a club in southern California, however, so I was able to take my citizenship exam in Los Angeles. I proudly displayed my knowledge of American history and the other areas I had studied, and because sexual orientation is not a measure in California of whether someone will be a good citizen, there were no obstacles there to my dream of becoming a United States citizen.

All that was left was my swearing in. I was ready. I had just won my fifth Wimbledon title (this time in doubles with Pam Shriver), and the U.S. Open—*my* new country's championship—was a few weeks away. All I had to do was remember the words to the Pledge of Allegiance.

I will never forget the ceremony. Standing with dozens of other new citizens, I had the same excited, overwhelming feeling I had when I read the Declaration of Independence, the Bill of Rights, and the U.S. Constitution when I loudly proclaimed: "I pledge allegiance to the flag of the United States of America . . ." and concluded, ". . . with liberty and justice for all."

That was 1981. I hadn't expected that fourteen years later I would be fighting for equality for women, gays, and lesbians. What will it take to dispel the myths and warped images people have about gender and sexual orientation?

I am a good citizen. I am proud to be an American. We live in the best country there is or will ever be. My candor about my sexuality has cost me millions of dollars in sponsorships and endorsements, but that's only money. I played my heart out on the tennis court, and that's what people wanted from me. Could I have played as well if I were living a lie? What would have happened if I had had to live in fear of someone "finding out" that I am a lesbian? What kind of athlete would I have been if I had felt someone was always looking over my shoulder—or in my bedroom window—so he or she could know whether to enforce a law that makes it all right to discriminate against me?

There are gays in all walks of life—doctors, lawyers, teachers, entertainers, construction workers, football players (gasp!), and yes, the military. But the gay part of a person is the private self. It affects only the individual and his or her partner. The public self—the doctor or garbage collector or whatever—is the essential portion on which we should assess the person's performance. In other words, is the person doing his or her job? That is what matters.

I am also a woman. To me, that does not mean I have two strikes against me, rather that I have two reasons for social activism. We all have our individual and civic reasons to speak out. Activism creates awareness and change. I can't be silent and just hope for the best. And neither can you.

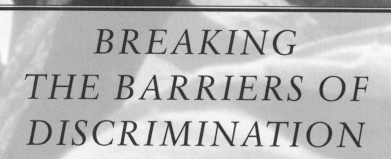

BREAKING
THE BARRIERS OF
DISCRIMINATION

MARY ADELIA ROSAMOND MCLEOD is the first female diocesan bishop of the Episcopal Church in the United States of America and the ninth bishop of Vermont. She attended the University of Alabama from 1956 to 1958 and received her L.Th. degree from the School of Theology, University of the South, in 1980. She holds honorary doctorates from the Episcopal Divinity School and Smith College. Prior to her election as Bishop of Vermont, McLeod and her husband were co-rectors of a church in Athens, Alabama, and of St. John's Episcopal Church in Charleston, West Virginia. McLeod serves on the board of visitors of the Episcopal Divinity School, and nationally on the board of pastoral development and the board of theological education.

A Gift of the Spirit

Mary Adelia Rosamond McLeod

My FATHER'S HOBBY was carpentry. He loved rubbing his hand over fine woods, mahogany, maple, redwood, and oak. He seemed happiest when he was in his woodworking shop shaping pieces of wood into salad bowls, napkin holders, desks, tables, and toy chests. He was a master at his work, never using nails, only the wooden pegs he had shaped and sanded. My father and I had wonderful conversations as his hands shaped pieces of wood begging to be furniture. He talked about his wood, what he was making, how it would last, and the feel of it. He spoke of life and recalled memories, telling me stories about our family. My father gave me a splendid gift in those long ago days, telling me I had good genes. My diary at the time I was ten years old reads:

> I am having a hard time with multiplication. I have to memorize all my ta-
> bles and I keep getting them all mixed up. Daddy was figuring up some

measurements for the table he is making. He knows how to multiply and doesn't even have to think about it. I told him I couldn't remember my tables like he can. He said I could because I have good memory genes. He tells me that a lot. Daddy says I can do anything I need to do because I have good genes. I guess my genes come from my family tree. Our family must be like a forest full of trees. When I need to do something important like multiplication the roots of my tree must get genes from the roots mixed with mine to help me. Daddy says I have smart genes and a lot of tenacity genes. Tenacity is a big word Daddy taught me and it means I keep on trying and am stubborn. Daddy said the tenacity genes mixed with my smart genes are the ones that are there to help me do anything I set my mind to.

Those long ago days of affirmation and inclusion in my father's workshop became latent gifts, buried deep within my soul as I grew up in the 1940s and entered a Southern world and a patriarchal church, both telling me tacitly that I could not do or be "anything I set my mind to." I could be a schoolteacher but not a principal. I could be a nurse but not a doctor. I could be a missionary but not a priest. My world was limited, though I did not know it. During those formative years, it did not occur to me to seriously question what girls could and could not do or be because I was a creature of my culture, which inundated me with the message that the most successful and fulfilled woman was one who married, had children, and devoted her life to raising those children and being a capable, loving, and industrious helpmate for her husband.

My naïveté fled as divorce instructed me in the brutal, unforgiving ways of second-class citizenship. My church confirmed my status. A sleeping forest stretched and yawned; a sapling reached through the compactness of the trees, seeking the sun for life.

My theology had not been shaped by my hands. The message of a lifetime was clear: the woman was created from the man; the woman's life was molded and patterned after the man's. The woman, in order to be happy, must be subservient to her father or her husband. It was God's perfect plan in ordering human lives.

SEEKING NEW PATHS

The sapling grew stronger, daring to nudge the branches of larger trees blocking the warmth of the life-giving sun. The questions poked through the density of the forest.

What of the other creation story in Genesis? "So God created humankind in God's image, in the image of God God created them; male and female God created them" (Genesis 1:27). In creation, did God give women genes inferior to those of men? No. If God created women and men in God's image, then women and men must be equal in order to accurately reflect God's image.

In my baptism, did God consider my gender problematic and therefore invest me with less of the Holy Spirit than my brothers? No. Paul speaks clearly of God's gift of the Spirit.

> Now there are varieties of gifts, but the same Spirit; and there are varieties of services, but the same Lord; and there are varieties of activities, but it is the same God who activates all of them in everyone. To each is given the manifestation of the Spirit for the common good. To one is given through the Spirit the utterance of wisdom, and to another the utterance of knowledge according to the same Spirit, to another faith by the same Spirit, to another gifts of healing by the one Spirit, to another the working of miracles, to another prophecy, to another the discernment of spirits, to another various kinds of tongues, to another the interpretation of tongues. All these are activated by one and the same Spirit, who allots to each one individually just as the Spirit chooses. For just as the body is one and has many members, and all the members of the body, though many, are one body, so it is with Christ. For in the one Spirit we were all baptized into one body—Jews or Greeks, slaves or free—and we were all made

to drink of one Spirit. Indeed, the body does not consist of one member but of many [I Corinthians 12:4–14].

The gift of the Spirit cannot be restricted nor measured.

Did God welcome the ministry of all the baptized and then place restrictions on women's exercise of the gifts of ministry? No. Each time I reaffirm my faith through the Baptismal Covenant, I along with other women and men promise, in the words of *The Book of Common Prayer*, "to proclaim by word and example the Good News of God in Christ, to seek and serve Christ in all persons, loving your neighbor as yourself strive for justice and peace among all people, and respect the dignity of every human being." There are no restrictions.

The Apostle Paul eloquently states: "But now that faith has come, we are no longer subject to a disciplinarian, for in Christ Jesus you are all children of God through faith. As many of you as were baptized into Christ have clothed yourselves with Christ. There is no longer Jew or Greek, there is no longer slave or free, there is no longer male and female; for all of you are one in Christ Jesus" (Galatians 3:25–28). It has become very clear to me that my God, our God, is inclusive and calls all human beings, regardless of religious tradition, gender, national origin, or sexual orientation to be agents of God's love and to be reconcilers in a hurt and broken world.

The sapling grew into a tree, the roots twisting and turning beneath the soil seeking new paths, tender new boughs reaching for God's heaven, for new life, for nameless hopes and dreams: "You have good genes; you can do anything you want to do if you set your mind to it."

A life of conditioning raised fearful facts and questions. My five children and my husband needed me at home, not out somewhere seeking life elsewhere. I did not need to earn a living. By the world's standards, I had everything I needed to be content and fulfilled: healthy children, loving husband, enough money, good friends, a niche in an affluent suburb. Why was I not satisfied when I had everything? What was the gnawing ache deep within my soul? Was I a rough piece of mahogany in God's workshop begging to be shaped into something beautiful? Was I being called by God to be something more?

I knew only that deep within my soul I was yearning to be who I was created to be, whatever that happened to be. No one thing could fill that aching place in my soul; no one person could meet that particular longing. One late afternoon, caught walking in the midst of a raging storm, with howling winds screaming at me and torrents of rain pelting my face, I knew I would know no peace until I responded to what I believed was God's call to be a priest.

ENTERING A MAN'S WORLD

I entered the strange and exhilarating world of seminary, one of two women in my class. In the Episcopal Church, the process for ordination is long and arduous. A person seeking ordination must first be named as a Postulant for Holy Orders. In order to receive that lofty designation, one must meet with and receive the approval of the governing body of the parish, submit to extensive psychological, psychiatric, and academic testing, and be approved at the diocesan level by the Commission on Ministry and the bishop. Most people entering seminary were postulants. I was not.

The Commission on Ministry, along with the bishop, felt it was imperative that I complete a year at seminary to test my academic abilities. Even though the testing indicated I would have no trouble with master's level courses, the fact remained that I had not completed college, and therefore my abilities were suspect. At the end of that first year, I was second in my class academically and prepared to return to the bishop and commission for the coveted status of postulant.

Sexism then reared its ugly and insidious head. By word of mouth, I learned that the commission and bishop were inclined to believe that if I was so smart, I couldn't possibly be pastoral. Therefore, my request for postulancy most likely would be denied.

Eve and the snake loomed large, coiling about my tree to squeeze the life out of me, invading my roots to stunt my growth, but the soil around my tree trunk and roots were fertilized with God's gracious gifts of smart and tenacious genes.

If I was to enter a man's world and be an ordained person in a patriarchal system, then I needed a powerful man's help. The dean of the seminary, the Very Reverend Urban Tigner Holmes agreed to become my advocate. Meeting with my bishop and me, Dean Holmes told the bishop that if he would not assist me in gaining postulancy, Dean Holmes would find me a bishop who would. There was no question in the dean's mind that I would, and indeed should, be ordained as a priest of the church. Several months later, I was made a postulant in my home diocese. A year later, I was made a candidate and then ordained deacon and priest in 1980.

The journey toward ordination was rife with sexism and exclusion that sought to undermine my dignity and my worth as an equal in the church. Over and over, I heard overtly and covertly that "women need not apply," "women are not wanted here," "women take jobs from men," "women cannot accurately reflect God's image," "women cannot be icons of Christ."

Almost as hurtful, bewildering, and frustrating, I had no female models. There was no woman to whom I could turn to ask questions about the craziness of it all. I felt alone, as if my tree had been transplanted to some hostile desert, near an oasis but not a part of it.

It was extremely difficult for women to be deployed in those early days of the ordination of women. (The canons of the Episcopal Church had been emended at the General Convention of 1976, allowing women to be ordained beginning January 1, 1977.) I had an additional and unique problem in that my husband had been ordained a priest in 1979 and could easily be deployed. The bishop was not prepared to deal with joint deployment. He arranged interviews for my husband and told me I could "tag along." Rather than actively helping me find a job, he told me he "would bless anything" I "could find." I hasten to add that after the meeting in the dean's office, the bishop had been supportive insofar as he was able; blessing anything I could find was better treatment than many women encountered.

Congregations in the South had not experienced women as priests, and most of them did not care to do so. It was not advantageous for any bishop, particularly a Southern bishop, to force a woman upon a congregation. In saying this, I do not affirm the actions of the bishop in any way; I merely explain the temper of the times. After we had been interviewed at several places, St. Timothy's Church in Athens, Alabama, issued a call to my husband and me as co-rectors. Three years later, we were called to be the co-rectors of St. John's Church in Charleston, West Virginia.

THE FIRST WOMEN BISHOPS

The late summer of 1985 in Anaheim, California, was hot and humid as the church gathered for the General Convention of that year. The spirit of that convention was one of excitement and anticipation as we were electing a new presiding bishop for a twelve-year term. Edmond Browning, bishop of Hawaii, was elected; to a standing ovation, he said, "There will be no outcasts in this Church."

A glorious new day had burst upon the horizon and with it the magnificent gifts of intentional inclusion and of honoring the gifts and dignity of every human being. There was a place for women; for gays and lesbians; for African Americans, Hispanics, and Asians; for the complete multicolored quilt of God's creatures.

As if to echo and affirm Bishop Browning's clarion call, the Diocese of Massachusetts elected a dynamic African American woman as bishop suffragan in 1988. Bishop-elect Barbara Harris became the first woman to be elected bishop in the Episcopal Church and also in the Anglican Communion.

The press and some of our dioceses were not kind to bishop-elect Harris. There were attempts to denigrate her abilities and worth; her life was threatened; some said they would leave the church if she were consecrated and ordained a bishop. The voices were angry and mean-spirited. The real meaning of inclusivity in our church was being tested. Women could be priests, but a woman as bishop was a different matter. The fabric of that all-male bastion the House of Bishops was about to be changed forever. And along with that change came the perception that the governance and structure of the church would also undergo radical change, resulting in irreparable harm and chaos. Nevertheless, after seven painful months, bishop-elect Barbara Harris was consecrated and ordained bishop. Four years later, Jane Holmes Dixon was elected bishop suffragan of the Diocese of Washington, D.C.

Watching these ordinations from afar gave me great joy and hope. At last, women were taking their rightful place in the councils of the church. However, one more step—a gigantic one—was needed: a woman had yet to be elected diocesan bishop in our country. The Anglican Church in New Zealand had elected Penelope Jamieson diocesan bishop, but our church appeared unable or unwilling to elect a woman diocesan. The Episcopal Church in the United States seemed to be saying that women could be elected as suffragans or assistants to diocesan bishops but could not be elected to head a diocese.

During those exciting times, I remained in West Virginia as a parish priest and archdeacon. My life was full and rich in a socially active urban parish, ministering to the working poor, street people, and those who had fallen through the cracks in our society and to the parishioners at St. John's. I had visions of remaining among those people until retirement.

However, I did allow my name to be submitted to several dioceses to stand for election as suffragan, co-adjutor, or diocesan bishop. It was important to me that women be in the elections and especially in diocesan bishop elections. I viewed my participation in diocesan bishop elections as a ministry of trailblazing for the woman who would finally be elected diocesan bishop. My generation of ordained women would not be elected, I thought, but among the new wave of ordained women, one would become a diocesan bishop.

I was wrong. The Diocese of Vermont made history on June 5, 1993, when the Electing Convention voted on the third ballot to elect a woman as diocesan bishop. I am that woman.

The responsibility of being the first woman diocesan bishop is awesome and burdensome. Being a symbol of hope and a voice for women in many religious traditions does not rest easily or lightly on me. God help me if I confuse the adulation of the symbol with the real person residing within. It is ever before me that the symbol is invested in my person, but it is not me.

Many people speak to me with great excitement about the pomp and glory and power of my position. My life is not all pomp, glory, and power; it is difficult and prayerful work. It is a life of hard decisions; of long hours as mediator, teacher, preacher, and pastor; of the tedium of administrative details; of innumerable meetings; of endless driving to visit fifty congregations regularly; of limited time with my husband; of encounters with sexism; of responsibility for the life and well-being of the church in Vermont; of advocating for the clergy; and of enabling programs and ministry.

It is also rewarding as I make visitations, watching people grow in their sense of ministry, sharing in the creativity of so many, walking with others as they struggle with the tough issues of life, cheering as programs of education unfold, providing funds, celebrating as new people come into the church, weeping and laughing with God's people. It is a good and fulfilling life, molded and shaped by God's grace and love.

THE GIFT OF NEW LIFE

I sit in the House of Bishops, where inclusiveness is not a reality. After twenty years, we still argue and discuss the validity of the ordination of women; we debate the issues inherent in human sexuality, tacitly avoiding full inclusion of our homosexual sisters and brothers. It is sometimes painful, sometimes overwhelming, and takes an incredible amount of energy to sit in that house with so many men. I believe the task of the members of the House of Bishops, as the elected leaders of the Episcopal Church, is to affirm the fact that we are all different and that our incredibly diverse gene pool is a blessing. We all have different opinions and ideas. The crucial questions before the church are: Can we differ without disliking? Can we be independent without excluding? Can we contradict without condemning? Can we deliberate without ill will?

We had better, for the sake of the One who breathed life into us. When we stand naked before the judgment seat of God, the question will not be, "Did you understand the mystery of who I am and whip everybody else into shape?" No, I believe God will simply ask, "Did you love me above all else, and did you show that love by loving your brothers and sisters as you loved yourself? Did you accept and forgive? Did you act with compassion, justice, and mercy for the benefit of others for my sake?"

My hope for the Church is strong and confident. For my hope rests where the Christian hope must always dwell. Not in ourselves but in the Christ who died for us, in the Christ who rose for us, in the Christ who loves and lives for us.

Because we believe in the Christ we have never seen, we may well learn to love, accept, and serve the Christs we see each day. Our very lives depend on it. Although I write from a Christian perspective, I do not wish to imply that I exclude other faith traditions from God's plan to reconcile all human beings to God's self.

A long and arduous journey it has been from my father's workshop to the Diocese of Vermont, one without road maps or a clear sense of direction. The sapling of long ago is a tree older and wiser, with broken limbs gnarled and misshapen, scarred branches, and a trunk with holes bored by woodpeckers allowing the sap to bleed, and yet a tree gloriously alive, firmly rooted, bending in the wind, lifting its arms to the heart of God, seeking life.

God's gift of new life never ends. God's gift of inclusivity never ends. My task is to love others as God loves me, by respecting the dignity of every human being and using my office as a gift to bring about more justice and peace in this small corner of the world called Vermont.

BEVERLY J. HARVARD is police chief for the City of Atlanta, the
first and still the only African American woman to run a major
U.S. police department. Beginning her law enforcement career
in 1974 as a patrol officer walking a beat, she became the first
Atlanta female officer assigned to the department's Executive
Protection Unit and the first to graduate from the FBI National
Academy. Her board service includes the International Associa-
tion of Chiefs of Police, Commission on Accreditation for Law
Enforcement Agencies, U.S. Attorney General's Working Group
on Reducing Violence in America, and Council on Battered
Women. She is a graduate of Morris Brown College, which
awarded her an honorary Doctor of Laws, and she holds an
M.S. degree in urban government and administration from
Georgia State University.

Turning the World Rightside Up

BEVERLY J. HARVARD

*H*ISTORICALLY, MANY WOMEN'S ISSUES and concerns have not been addressed until women exerted themselves to influence the course of events. Our history tells us of those early pioneers and of other strong and valiant women who have spoken out. I think of women like Abigail Smith Adams, Susan B. Anthony, Sandra Day O'Connor, Aileen Fernandez, Shirley Chisholm, Mary McLeod Bethune, Geraldine Ferraro, the women of Desert Storm, Janet Reno, Toni Morrison, Hillary Clinton, Rosa Parks, Coretta Scott King, and Cynthia McKinney.

Most of these women came from different backgrounds, pursued different causes, and had different goals. Yet the common thread that I see throughout their lives is one of self-sacrifice. It is a willingness to give of oneself.

As the years have gone on, woman has touched the most vital fields in our civilization. Wherever she has contributed, she has left the mark of a strong character. She has nursed and molded her children's minds, conduct, and deportment. The educational institutions she has established and directed have met the needs of her young people. Her cultural development has concentrated itself into artistic presentation. She is successful as a poet and novelist. She is shrewd in business and capable in politics. She recognizes the importance of uplifting others through social, civic, and religious activities.

Frederick Douglass once made a plea that the African American not be judged by the heights to which he or she has risen, but by the depths from which he or she has climbed. Similarly, the true worth of a people must be measured by the character of its womanhood.

Too often women are stereotyped as less assertive or more emotional than men, less mathematical or more artistic, less persuasive or more sensitive, less open or more introspective, or any one of a hundred similar generalities without foundation. Women are expected to be tough but cannot be macho, or they are expected to take responsibility but also to follow advice.

My personal responsibility as a female executive in the criminal justice system is to dispel such *myths* and to get on with the business of managing. Recently the Atlanta Police Department, which is no longer a workforce dominated by "good ole boys," placed a significant number of women in nontraditional roles. Now more than ever, women are in top positions. Did that come about by accident? Of course not. But let there be no mistake about it. There are no free rides. Any woman hired or elevated in corporate or public service America has to be the best. In some respects, these women have to be even better than the best.

As a police chief, and particularly as a female police chief, I feel privileged to be in a leadership role, responsible for maintaining peace and safety in our city. However, this responsibility does involve a lot of hard work, many long hours, numerous sacrifices, and a very lonely place at the top at times. Yet, it never occurred to me not to pursue my dreams because I am a woman.

As the year 2000 approaches, more and more jobs will open to women. But we must be trained to fill those jobs and have the confidence to seek out nontraditional occupations. We need to ensure that women are given equal opportunities in education and employment.

Moreover, children and adults must have the opportunity to learn about the true historical roles and the many accomplishments of women from all walks of life. Although they are good starts, it is not enough to observe Black History Month or National Women's History Month once a year. Only through continual education and awareness will the expectations of women and men match the realities of the world we live in today. We also must be especially concerned with how we prepare our young women to grapple with challenges and become leaders who will pave the way for others to follow. To accomplish these goals, we must promote the following: a sense of self-confidence, communication skills, connectedness with other women, a commitment to action, the significance of service, and the power of both men and women working together to change the world for the good of all mankind.

We must educate our female students by giving them the appropriate survival kits of knowledge and experience to enhance their self-confidence and their love of learning. We must work to keep their self-esteem high. We must help them reach their fullest potential and become competent resourceful women. We must reach girls in the early grades, communicating to them that they can be whatever they want to be by daring to be the best.

Let me remind you that as women we have the right to have our voices heard economically, politically, and socially. We have the right to try to remove restrictions that discriminate.

The voices of women from our past and our present continue to be in the forefront of every major progressive social change movement in American history: voices that secured the rights of suffrage and equal opportunities, voices in the abolitionist movement, the emancipation movement, the industrial labor movement, the civil rights movement, the women's liberation movement, the law and order movement, and the environmental movement. Women of America, let us join those voices and commit ourselves to a greater voice in participation for all members of society, without regard to gender.

As we commemorate the 75th anniversary of woman suffrage and the founding of the League of Women Voters, I am reminded of the groundbreaking accomplishments of our foremothers and foresisters and of the many options available to American women today.

Those seventy-five years should remind us of the strength and perseverance of women, our Rock of Ages. We, and the generations of women after us, have the obligation to continue confronting all obstacles placed in the road to full participation and equality. The doll-baby woman is a thing of the past and the wide-awake woman is forging ahead, prepared for all emergencies and ready to answer any call, even if it is to face cannons on the battlefield. In the words of Sister Sojourner Truth at the 1851 women's rights convention in Akron, "If the first woman God ever made was strong enough to turn the world upside down all alone, women together ought to be able to turn it rightside up again." America, that's what women headed toward the twenty-first century are going to do: their Contract with America is to turn the world rightside up.

But in turning the world rightside up, we must continue to be mindful of the fact that our struggle is far from over. Seventy-five years after we received the vote, we still need to raise our voices in support of affordable health and child care, adequate housing, affirmative action, and reduced teen pregnancy, and in opposition to sexual harassment, spousal abuse, and domestic violence.

Yes, the voices of our past have taught us to believe in a future where women will help make the rules, create the policies, and pass the laws about issues that affect Americans every day. There is no question in my mind that a huge reservoir of untapped talent is present throughout the public and private sector and also in the homes of America: that resource is *America's dynamic woman*.

A living example of the struggles and sacrifices of so many that have gone before me, I now have the opportunity to head one of the major police departments in this country. I offer a special salute to America's dynamic woman. I am honored to be able to share in her story.

ADA E. DEER is assistant secretary of Indian affairs in the Department of the Interior. From 1977 to 1993, she was senior lecturer at the School of Social Work and American Indian Studies Program at the University of Wisconsin at Madison. Deer was elected the first woman chair of the Menominee following her work as vice president and lobbyist for the National Committee to Save the Menominee People and Forest in 1972 to 1973. She has served on numerous national boards, including the Girl Scouts of America, Housing Assistance Council, Rural America, Common Cause, the Native American Rights Fund, the Independent Sector, and the Council on Foundations. A graduate of the University of Wisconsin, which has awarded her an honorary D.H.L., she holds an M.S.W. degree from Columbia University and is a former fellow of the Institute of Politics at Harvard's Kennedy School of Government.

Or You Can Get to Work

ADA E. DEER

I AM NOT OLD ENOUGH to remember when women could not vote, but my mother most certainly was. It is because of her that I make advocacy and activism the center of my life. She always told me that I was not put on this earth to enjoy myself but to help others. I still can hear her saying that to me, and I have tried to live my life according to that precept. I also guide my actions by the equally important principle that one person can make a difference.

When you look around this world, it is hard to believe that one person can make any kind of difference at all, but trust me, it can be done. I have seen it happen in my lifetime, and I am not finished yet!

I was born and raised in a log cabin on the banks of the Wolf River on the Menominee Indian Reservation in central Wisconsin. The Menominee Indian Reservation is a land of dense forests, a winding wild river, and streams and lakes that nourish the land, animals, and the people. I am an extension of this environment; it has fostered my growth and enriched my vision. Appreciation of and reverence for the land is *fundamental* to being an American Indian.

My mother was a public health nurse and a Quaker. She was the daughter of a wealthy mainline Philadelphia family, which disowned her when she married my Menominee father. Her first nursing job was in Appalachia. She was next sent to the Rosebud Sioux Reservation in South Dakota and then transferred to Menominee. There she met and married my father, a nearly full-blood Menominee with, as we say, just a squirt of French blood. My mother gave birth to nine children, five of whom lived. Our family of seven had no running water, electricity, telephone, or television. What we did have were the land and the Menominee culture. While all the statistics said we were poor, I never felt poor in spirit.

My mother placed great faith in the value of an education. It was a requirement for all her children. Throughout our childhoods, she exerted every effort and paid any price to assure us of a good education, including sending me to live in a different town. She was right. I won the only tribal scholarship to the University of Wisconsin at Madison, where I became its first Menominee graduate.

After college, I earned a master's degree in social work from Columbia University. I was drawn to social work because it embodies many Indian values and is dedicated to social justice and the elimination of discrimination. We students were taught to be advocates for those who were unable to advocate for themselves; we were asked to empower the powerless and to give voice to the voiceless. Social work is the perfect profession for someone like me.

After graduate school, I started my professional career in Minneapolis. I was a program director for a neighborhood house, a public school social worker, and a community services coordinator for the Bureau of Indian Affairs. I then became director of the Upward Bound program, and later director of the Program for Recognizing Individual

Determination Through Education (PRIDE) at the University of Wisconsin at Stevens Point.

I had entered law school when I was urged by other tribal members and my family to go home to help restore my tribe to federally recognized status. There was no choice: I left law school and returned to the reservation. Thus began one of the most compelling times of my life.

RESTORATION

In order to understand federal Indian policy, a brief explanation of our history is essential. The leaders of my tribe signed the Wolf River Treaty of 1854, guaranteeing the Menominee 250,000 acres of land *and sovereignty over that land—forever.* This was not a gift.

Under decisions delivered by a range of Supreme Court Justices, from Chief Justice John Marshall to members of the current Court, the Menominee, like other tribes, owned their land and much more *before* the treaty era. In the treaties, we ceded most of our aboriginal land, held by us for thousands of years, but we reserved a small part of it. Hence the term *reservation.* Our tribal leaders were sophisticated people. They insisted upon land, sovereignty, and federal trust protection from the onrushing settlers. In that time of crisis, one of the greatest collisions of cultures in the history of the world, our leaders relied upon these promises.

Of course, promise after promise was broken. By the end of the treaty-making period in 1871, tribes held only 140 million acres, a tiny fraction of their original holdings. But the non-Indians marching west wanted more, and so the General Allotment Act of 1887 was passed. Indian land was opened for wholesale homesteading, and by the 1930s, the tribal land base had dwindled to 50 million acres.

The next major assault on our land and sovereignty took place under the termination policy of the 1950s. In 1954, Congress terminated the federal relationship with the Menominee. Termination was a misguided and now discredited federal policy. It severed all ties between the tribes and the government; it unraveled the special relationship that was guaranteed by treaty when Indian land was ceded throughout American history. This new policy not only broke treaty law but also aimed at assimilating Indians into the "mainstream" culture.

Soon after termination, the Menominee Tribe began to lose its identity. In contrast to its prosperous past, Menominee County became Wisconsin's newest, smallest, and poorest county. Although people fought termination, the results were shattering: land was sold to pay newly imposed taxes, the tribal economy was wrecked, the hospital was closed, reservation life was devastated, and our culture and spiritual life were being destroyed. My time for active tribal involvement had arrived.

There was only one way to save five thousand years of history: the tribe had to force a reversal of the federal government's termination policy. Politics—that is, a campaign—was the route to reestablishing the tribe. Politics had gotten us into this mess; politics was also the way to get out of it. The Menominee collectively discovered the kind of determination that human beings find only in times of impending destruction. Against all odds, we invented a new policy—restoration.

A group of us organized tribal supporters and reached out to likeminded supporters across the nation. I went to Washington to lobby members of the U.S. House and Senate. I never gave up. Persuading opinion makers and powerful people who could help became my way of life. Persistence paid off: on December 22, 1973, President Nixon signed the Menominee Restoration Act.

Passage of this act marked the first time both Congress and the president reversed themselves on federal Indian policy. It also was the beginning of the end for the policy of termination. This restorative legislation is a vivid reminder of how great a government can be when it is large enough to admit and rectify its mistakes. It is also indicative of my tribe's spirit, tenacity, and ability to hold other sovereign entities accountable. While my tribe has rebuilt itself, other tribes are still fighting for restoration.

Termination was a horrible, decimating policy that few people thought would ever be reversed. The lesson I learned in the fight was to forge ahead; one person can move mountains.

AFTER RESTORATION

After restoration, I became the first woman chair of the Menominee Tribe as it began the process of spiritual as well as physical restoration. I am proud to say that today the tribe is strong and functioning well. In the last few years, it completed buying back much of the land it was forced to sell during the termination period.

My experience during the restoration fight showed me firsthand that the political process can work. In 1977, I joined the faculty of my alma mater in Madison as a lecturer. About that time, I also truly began my avocation of partisan politics.

One day, as I was speaking to the executive director of the Wisconsin Democratic Party about involving more Indians, she asked why I didn't become a candidate myself. She had a point. Running for office seemed to be a natural progression for me. So in both 1978 and 1982, I ran in Wisconsin for secretary of state. In each campaign, I came in second in the primary, but that was still extraordinary for an American Indian woman.

In 1991, dissatisfied with the representation my district was receiving, I ran for the U.S. House of Representatives from Wisconsin's Second District. This was a huge undertaking. I am a woman of color with no independent means, and I refused to accept political action committee money. As Shirley Chisholm said, referring to her own 1972 presidential campaign, I was "unbossed and unbought." In the primary, I ran against the most heavily financed challenger in the country and beat him. However, I could not beat the incumbent in the eight short weeks of the general election campaign.

After the 1992 election, I was buoyed by the expectation that the new administration would bring real change to the nation; I wanted to be part of it. President Clinton promised an administration that looked like America. There I was, an American Indian, a woman, a social worker. So after another campaign, I returned to Washington as a high-level policy maker at the Department of the Interior, where I believe that I can make a difference as an advocate and voice for Indians and women.

GETTING TO WORK

When I look around at our society, I am infuriated at the problems we, the inhabitants of the richest and most powerful nation in the world, still have. For example, women continue to suffer discrimination in the workplace, and the condition of Indian health is appalling.

Remember, the Equal Pay Act was signed into law by President Kennedy in 1963! Yet women still make only seventy-one cents for every dollar that men make. That is an improvement over the fifty-nine cents of the early 1980s, but it is not nearly enough.

The federal government's Glass Ceiling Commission, in its 1995 report *Good for Business: A Strategic Plan to Make Full Use of the Nation's Human Capital,* stated that women now account for 46 percent of the labor force but only 5 percent of the top corporate jobs. In 1990, women's median annual wages were $12,250, and men's were $21,522. Women with college degrees are paid $10,000 per year less than men with the same level of education. These numbers are unacceptable!

In the sphere of Indian health, the situation is even worse. Statistics show the state of Indian health to be deplorable, clearly indicating a waste of human potential. While the United States has made progress in reducing the incidence of infant and maternal mortality, Indian women live considerably shorter lives than non-Indian women. Many more Indians die of diabetes, tuberculosis, suicide, alcoholism, accidents, and homicides than do the rest of the population. Indian educational levels are lower than those for the society at large, and unemployment and poverty are endemic. Health care and preventive care problems may be greatest for American Indians and Alaska Natives, but all minority groups in America share these mean consequences of poverty.

When we look to the future, we think most of all about our young people. Each night, tens of thousands of girls and boys across Indian country go to sleep. Some in my Wisconsin homeland hear the vibrant sounds I heard many years ago in the cabin where I grew up. Others hear the wind in the Douglas fir trees at Warm Springs, the surging current of the great Missouri at Fort Peck, or the song of the canyon wren calling out from a red rock monument at Navajo. There is no reason why they cannot grow up to live in prosperity, in good health, with excellent educations, in clean environments, and immersed in their rich traditions.

In considering all these issues, you can do one of two things. You can throw up your hands and declare that the problems are too big to solve, or you can get to work. Clearly everything cannot be solved at once, but you have to start. Teach someone to read. Make sure you vote in every election and encourage your friends and colleagues to do the same. Run for office. Women candidates win as often as men, but first a woman has to run. Don't agonize, organize.

In 1993, I addressed the first major conference held at the Carrie Chapman Catt Center for Women and Politics at Iowa State University. Catt graduated from Iowa State in 1880; the new center is a wonderful tribute to her struggle. As I was surrounded by women candidates, it occurred to me that the dream of at least 50 percent representation by women in the U.S. House and Senate and in state and local offices could be achieved sooner than I had hoped. I also found it very easy in that setting to imagine a woman as president or vice president of the United States.

Now we all have to work even harder to make that dream come true.

Carrie Chapman Catt put it this way in a 1921 commencement address at Iowa State:

To the wrongs that need resistance,
To the right that needs assistance,
To the future in the distance,
Give yourselves.

SOURCES OF STRENGTH

In order to keep your spirits up, you need to draw upon your own sources of strength. I have two major sources of strength to keep me going in difficult times. One is my mother and her background. She bore with her the Quaker tradition of peaceful activism to achieve justice as well as her personal dedication to improving the lives of others. On my father's side, I have my tribal heritage with its love of the land and the animals and my sense of community and connectedness to the tribe as well as to women in many other tribes.

This wonderful traditional Taos poem was sent to me on a postcard:

I am a woman,
I hold up half of the sky,
I am a woman,
I nourish half of the earth,
I am a woman,
The rainbow touches my shoulders,
The universe encircles my eyes.

(Actually we all know it's more than half!)
Draw your strength from this poem.

We all can do more than we ever dreamed; we simply need to act and to keep acting. Don't ever give up. One person can change the world!

DIANE C. YU is general counsel of the State Bar of California. From 1986 to 1987, she was a White House Fellow, serving as special assistant to the U.S. Trade Representative, Executive Office of the President. She served as superior court commissioner in the Alameda County Superior Court from 1983 to 1987, was an attorney in private practice from 1977 to 1983, and taught English at Tunghai University in Taiwan from 1973 to 1974. She serves on the American Bar Association Accreditation Committee, Commission on Women in the Profession, and Multicultural Women Attorneys Network Nominating Committee. Her board memberships include Chinese for Affirmative Action, California Consortium to Prevent Child Abuse, and the Commonwealth Club of California. She is a graduate of Oberlin College and the University of California at Berkeley Boalt Hall School of Law.

Gender, Race, and Democracy

DIANE C. YU

*I*F IT WERE NOT for American democracy, I would not be here. My parents came from China to the United States and Great Britain to advance their medical studies in the mid 1940s. Although they had never intended to stay in the West permanently, they eventually did so upon the advice of their concerned families as their homeland fell to Communist armies and the new government repudiated freedom and individual rights.

I cannot imagine what it would have been like to have been born and raised under a totalitarian regime rather than in America. Virtually everything in my life would have been different. The musings that follow are my attempt to express my thoughts on democracy in America, its influence on certain of my life decisions, and the challenges facing it as we approach the new millennium.

BEGINNINGS

In two respects, my start in life was not entirely auspicious. First, I was supposed to be a boy. My parents were Chinese from the mainland and had already had one daughter three years before. Therefore, I was the designated masculine offspring, intended to carry on the family name pursuant to ancient Chinese cultural norms. Suffice it to say that I ended up with two more sisters before my folks decided that four girls were enough.

Second, I was born on Christmas Day. As anyone whose birthday falls at the end of the year knows only too well, there is a distinct disadvantage to such timing. For the first twelve years of my life—when such things truly mattered—I always heard the unwelcome words, "This is for both," indicating that I was getting a combined birthday and Christmas present. My sisters got two gifts, so to me, it was an equity issue; I learned quickly that life is unfair. Some psychologists would probably say that this circumstance triggered an early interest in the justice system on my part.

Notwithstanding these two strikes against me, I cannot credibly complain about my childhood. My three sisters and I all did well in school and were nicknamed "The Yu Dynasty" as a result of our extended success in scholarship and extracurricular activities.

As for my view of democracy, as with nearly all things important to me, it originated with my parents. My mother and father had settled in Rochester, New York, where my father began an illustrious career in cardiology. Among his many accomplishments was election to the presidencies of the New York State Heart Assembly and the American Heart Association. Often I would hear him say that only in the United States could a foreign-born foreign-trained immigrant attain such high posts. Once in a while, he expressed some regret at not being able to see his family and friends in China again (he died in 1991 without having been back to China), but then he would be quick to emphasize how much better life was in America. I know it was a matter of key significance to him that his children were growing up in America; he did not take the advantages we enjoyed here for granted.

My mother was also a great inspiration. In the late 1950s and 1960s, two-career couples were rare. My mother was therefore a true pioneer: a Chinese immigrant woman doctor in an overwhelmingly male-dominated profession. She, without role models and lacking societal or networking support, managed to succeed in a demanding profession *and* raise a family. Although I am ashamed to admit it, there were times in my childhood when I selfishly wished she had eschewed her medical career and devoted all her efforts to the family. Yet, simultaneously, I was proud of her intelligence and achievements and hopeful that someday I, too, would do worthwhile things with my ability and education. Watching her persuaded me that women were just as capable as men in terms of handling a career. It also lent support to my conviction that America was indeed a land of opportunity for all.

Consequently, not only did my parents set an example for me in terms of character, integrity, and excellence, but they also conveyed their abiding belief in the democratic system. Without question, they were grateful to be here, in a free country, and to have a chance to become American citizens. It was a touchstone for their existence. It became one for mine.

That inclination translated into a keen interest on my part in American history, government, and policy making and ultimately in the legal system (the latter distantly attributable to my mother's favorite television show, *Perry Mason,* and directly related to the absence of math on the Law School Admission Test; but I get ahead of myself).

A MINORITY WOMAN IN AMERICA

Representative Barbara Jordan made this statement on July 25, 1974, as a member of the Committee on the Judiciary in the House of Representatives during the debate on the Articles of Impeachment:

"We, the people." It is a very eloquent beginning. But when that document was completed on the seventeenth of September in 1787 I was not included in that "We, the people." I felt somehow for many years that George Washington and Alexander Hamilton just left me out by mistake. But through the process of amendment, interpretation and court decision I have finally been included in "We, the people."

In the mid fifties, when my parents wanted to move out of the center of the city to a more affluent Rochester neighborhood, they first had to obtain the permission of the suburban white families who lived there. As I was growing up, I frequently ran into people who saw my Asian face and assumed that I was a foreigner. They would inquire where I came from. They would ask how long I had been here. They would even comment on how well I spoke English. When I told them the truth, some were startled, some were embarrassed, and some were upset. Often I would get a pat on the head, a "There, there," as if to say that they knew I had made it all up, but it was all right.

I remember how kids from other neighborhoods—not mine, thankfully—would occasionally taunt me by calling me "slant eyes" or "Chink" or "Jap." At first, I could not understand why they bothered to do that since I had done nothing to offend them. Fairly quickly I caught on that some people disliked Asians or Asian Americans on principle and wanted me to know that. One reason I selected Oberlin College was because it was the first college in the United States to accept persons regardless of race, sex, creed, or national origin. I thought it would be a hospitable environment in which to learn, and it was.

But later on, in business and professional settings, I would sometimes encounter condescension or indifference—more sophisticated manifestations of hostility and prejudice. It did not matter one whit who I was, where I grew up, how well educated I was, what talents I might have, or what potential I possessed. What mattered was simply my race or gender or both. That was a powerful message.

The 1990s experience of being a woman of color in America is a more subtle but just as invidious replay of the "getting permission" drill to which my parents had been subjected nearly forty years ago. Racism, sexism, and other forms of bias and discrimination are persistent and pervasive weeds in our democratic garden. Like many women, I have encountered disbelievers who resent competence and assertiveness when passivity and subservience would be more comforting to them. Like members of many other minority groups, I have winced when "qualified" is inserted (as it almost always is) before the word "minority," ever reminding us that qualifications among us are seen to be the exception and not the rule. It becomes as tiresome, if not outright demeaning, to be constantly "surprising" people with what I can do as it is to be ignored as invisible and inconsequential.

I therefore have reached the conclusion that being a member of a racial minority and a woman has given me little choice but to work harder than my peers to achieve comparable results and recognition. That is more an observation than a complaint, in part because my parents' life-styles had prepared me for long hours. Certainly I acknowledge the benefits conferred on me by my parents in the form of good genes and a positive outlook. I also recognize that on occasion it is a distinct advantage to be a woman and minority because I can appreciate and empathize with a wider universe of people. In the final analysis, despite the drawbacks, I would not have it any other way.

BECOMING A LAWYER

Probably my most decisive response to the injustices and undemocratic conditions I encountered was to choose a career in the law. Several mentors and Oberlin professors whom I consulted about my future career had recommended the law because in that course of study I could gain the knowledge, expertise, wherewithal, and opportunity to become a constructive force for necessary change. They knew how important issues of racial harmony, fairness, and justice for all persons were to me; my becoming a lawyer would legitimize my mission.

An additional consideration was my personal temperament: I was too much a Confucian moderate to be a convincing radical, but I was also too mindful of my own and my family's history to sit back and let others carry the load of reform alone. Gaining an understanding of the law and how it works was also a natural extension of my early interest in American history, politics, and government, all of which are heavily shaped by the legal principles and the balance-of-power relationships that have evolved since the Founding Fathers first put quill to paper.

Moreover, law seemed to be an appropriate outlet for my verbal tendencies. (As I have noted, I considered the absence of math on the LSAT a definite plus!) Law also afforded me a chance to follow in my mother's footsteps and be a pathfinder, since there were very few women attorneys in the late 1970s, the time when I finished law school. Finally, it seemed to be an honorable profession (although in recent years, assaults on the power, privileges, and occasional excesses of the bar are on the rise and are rendering law practice less desirable).

Notwithstanding all these positive rationales, I really had no clue what I was getting into when I sent in my law school applications and ultimately enrolled in law school at the University of California at Berkeley. I had never met a lawyer in my life and was completely ignorant of the rigors and realities of the modern-day legal academy. Taiwan had been my home for the preceding two years; I had been studying Chinese language and literature in anticipation of pursuing a Ph.D. in Chinese poetry—hardly the best preparation for civil procedure, crimes, and torts. Yet somehow I made it through, culture shock and all.

My innocence made me fearless when it came to the job search. I had no idea how novel an Asian American woman lawyer appeared to others at that time, so job interviews where I was questioned about Chinese restaurants and kung fu instead of my background and qualifications did give me pause. Fortunately I landed a superb initial job with an Oakland law firm where high standards of ethics and professionalism were practiced daily. A new lawyer could not have had a better introduction to the legal profession. At present, I am the first woman, first minority, and youngest person ever to be appointed general counsel for the State Bar of California; I am the chief legal adviser for the entity governing the state's nearly 150,000 lawyers ("the lawyers' lawyer").

In any event, relatively early in my career I have experienced many highlights: arguing and winning a case before the U.S. Supreme Court, a rare and special event in the life of any lawyer; arguing dozens of cases before the California Supreme Court on behalf of the State Bar of California; being appointed a White House Fellow by the president and, as a special assistant to the U.S. trade representative, observing first-hand how the executive branch functions; being selected as the first Asian American California superior court commissioner, and one of the state's youngest such commissioners ever; and serving on numerous state and national professional boards and commissions. I have a definite public service bent, and my legal training and skills accord me both access to decision-making corridors and the ability to have an effect.

Furthermore, in light of my position within the California legal profession (which counts as its members more than one-seventh of all U.S. lawyers) and my heavy involvement in professional and civic activities, I am referred to as a role model for many young women attorneys, especially those from minority groups. Since I had very few female mentors when I started out, I am glad to give these women a sense that a career in law can be stimulating and fulfilling—if one is willing to put in some extra effort. Once again, I owe a debt to my parents, who early on demonstrated the beneficial effects that flow from high energy, dedication, and endurance.

WOMEN AND THE FUTURE OF DEMOCRACY

Abigail Smith Adams wrote the following to her husband, John, on June 17, 1782:

> Patriotism in the female sex is the most disinterested of all virtues. Excluded from honors and from offices, we cannot attach ourselves to the State or Government from having held a place of eminence. Even in the freest countries our property is subject to the control and disposal of our partners, to whom the laws have given a sovereign authority. Deprived of

a voice in legislation, obliged to submit to those laws which are imposed upon us, is it not sufficient to make us indifferent to the public welfare? Yet all history and every age exhibit instances of patriotic virtue in the female sex, which considering our situation equals the most heroic of yours.

It is currently fashionable to cite the unprecedented level of distrust in our government. Poverty, illiteracy, illegitimacy, inadequate health care, violence, and crime are worsening. Complicating matters further, rapid demographic changes are reshaping our society into a multicultural mosaic. In only a few years, the workplace and political environment will be startlingly different, almost unrecognizable. Even though these dislocations and uncertainties appear to have sprung up recently, they actually have been building for decades.

I have only a dim personal recollection of the fifties and early sixties, but the reputed wholesomeness and nostalgia of that period is forever captured in the ubiquitous situation comedies of those *Father Knows Best* days. We tend to forget, however, that serious problems were hidden from view: we had civility and personal security but no equality of opportunity or full extension of democratic benefits to all citizens.

It took the Supreme Court's 1954 ruling in *Brown* v. *Topeka Board of Education,* a host of other landmark cases, and a consensus-driven Congress acting in the aftermath of Kennedy's assassination to ensure a modicum of fairness and justice for all. The nonwhite and nonmale segments of the population began to exert their newly acquired rights and privileges to vote, improve their education, and compete for jobs in fields from which they had previously been barred. In the late sixties, they were joined by outspoken young people protesting what is now widely regarded as an ill-advised, if not immoral, war in Vietnam. We also had the very real threat of the Cold War and its offshoots, like bomb shelters and McCarthyism, as an ominous overlay to both foreign and domestic policy.

The decades of the 1970s and 1980s saw dramatic swings in the American public's mood and temperament, from cynicism and apathy in the post-Watergate era to confidence-boosting boom times in the 1980s, followed by a stomach-wrenching recession. As the pace and rate of change were rising, people began to feel they were losing control over their lives.

The 1990s have been characterized by growing pessimism as well as cognizance of the limits of growth and progress. In some ways, people have never been closer nor had more choices to consider, yet estrangement and stress levels reportedly are up, and satisfaction levels are down. In the face of fragmentation and discord in society, consensus is harder to achieve wherever one looks—in education, religion and morals, law, the media, business, race relations, international affairs, and domestic priorities.

We might well wonder whether we have moved from the conception and *creation* of American democracy, through the *preservation* and expansion of the Union, to a radical restructuring of our basic beliefs in our democratic system, all in little more than two centuries.

I am troubled that our society at present does not adhere enough to what Franklin D. Roosevelt, in his Second Inaugural Address, called "the test of our progress," which is not whether more is added to "the abundance of those who have much" but "whether we provide enough for those who have too little." We must not let short-term expedience, budget woes, a circle-the-wagons self-protective streak, or partisan cross fire multiply the misery. We need to take a longer view, for one of the distinguishing tenets of the American system is that government has the responsibility for safeguarding the rights of *all* its citizens.

If our nation is to survive into the next century with most of its founding principles intact, it has no alternative but to deal forthrightly with discrimination and prejudice. A true democracy cannot indulge in exclusion, intolerance, and bias without detracting from its credibility and support. We may not have devised the best tools to remedy the problem as yet, but we cannot and should not give up.

We can take some comfort in the notion that our present difficulties were perceived more than 150 years ago by Alexis de Tocqueville, who put this prescient warning in *Democracy in America:* "If I were called upon to predict the future, I should say that the abolition of slavery will, in the common course of things, increase the repugnance of the white population for the blacks. . . . The danger of a conflict between the white and the black inhabitants . . . perpetually haunts the imagination of the Americans, like a painful dream."

The findings of the 1968 Kerner Commission on the racially charged Watts riots in Los Angeles and the 1993 Christopher Commission on the "civil disturbances" following the failure to convict police officers charged with beating black motorist Rodney King offer more contemporary depictions of America's racial schism. We need to reinforce the concept of equal protection under the law as a means of attaining a society that is truly fair, colorblind, and gender neutral. We are not yet there.

I place a great deal of hope in the women of America to help us find our way back to our original democratic ideals. As Abigail Adams commented in her letter to her husband, the contributions of patriotic women to the public good and welfare may be overlooked when contrasted with the more obvious heroics of men, but they are equally weighty and honorable. I am counting on women to continue this long tradition and assert their rightful place in the policy-making arena. Minority women like myself have a particular need to come to the forefront of this effort because only we grapple with the dual burdens of racial and gender discrimination.

We are well equipped for the task. Women have more than a passing acquaintance with antiquated restrictive attitudes and policies that can hurt, inhibit, and bind. In addition, we must tackle such problems as a reluctance to succeed on the part of young girls and women in academic and other settings, because all women still must journey far before they can be confident that their merits will be given sufficient attention.

One case in point is the 1995 report of the Glass Ceiling Commission, *Good for Business: A Strategic Plan to Make Full Use of the Nation's Human Capital,* which exhaustively detailed how women, despite marked gains by white females in some quarters, are still conspicuously absent from many male bastions in business and industry. Ninety-five percent of senior management positions are held by white men, who constitute only 43 percent of the total workforce. The commission found that more than thirty years after the passage of the Civil Rights Act of 1964, stereotyped preconceptions and fears continue to flourish, blocking the pathways to promotion and leadership for women and persons of color.

It is up to women themselves, to a considerable extent, to ensure that meaningful progress is made to modify this landscape of privilege for some and exclusion of others. The days of women's passivity are gone. Still, it takes no genius to see that the *potential* abundance of resources, riches, and opportunities in the United States is without parallel. Hard work, ambition, talent, creativity, and personal skills can produce phenomenal rewards, for both men and women.

I remain a determined optimist, overall, about America's prospects and the future of democracy. President Lincoln said it best, in his First Inaugural Address, when he stated: "We must not be enemies. Though passion may have strained, it must not break our bonds of affection. The mystic chords of memory, stretching from every battlefield and patriot grave to every living heart and hearthstone, all over this broad land, will yet swell the chorus of the Union when again touched, as surely they will be, by the better angels of our nature."

For all of its manifest flaws, our political process vests ultimate decision-making power in its citizens. Through the right to vote, we control our political destiny. We also are entitled to participate in the development of public policy at the local, state, and national levels. In a genuine sense, we can choose to be activists for democracy. "All the ills of democracy can be cured by more democracy," as politician Alfred E. Smith commented once. I believe that is true.

In the meantime, we must all take part in the effort of renewal and restoration of real democracy in America. We must recapture "the better angels of our nature." Because if government is not going to be "of the people, by the people, for the people," then we have lost the most precious aspect of our national heritage.

NICOLE HOLLANDER is a cartoonist and illustrator. Her syndicated cartoon strip, *Sylvia*, appears in more than fifty daily and weekly newspapers, among them the *Boston Globe*, the *Chicago Tribune*, the *Detroit News*, the *Seattle Times*, and the *San Francisco Chronicle*. Thirteen collections of her cartoons have been published, including *Mercy, It's the Revolution and I'm in My Bathrobe!* (1982), *My Weight Is Always Perfect for My Height—Which Varies* (1982), *Never Tell Your Mother This Dream* (1985), *Everything Here Is Mine: Sylvia's Unhelpful Guide to Cat Behavior* (1992), and *Female Problems* (1995). She is a graduate of the University of Illinois and earned an M.F.A. degree from Boston University.

©1990 by Nicole Hollander

FAMILY, WORK, AND COMMUNITY

JUDY WOODRUFF is senior correspondent and anchor at CNN. She is former chief Washington correspondent for the *MacNeil/Lehrer NewsHour* (1983–1993) and anchor of *Frontline with Judy Woodruff* (1984–1990) on PBS. From 1970 to 1974, she reported on the Georgia state legislature and was news anchor for a CBS affiliate in Atlanta. In 1975, she joined NBC News as an Atlanta-based general assignment reporter. From 1977 to 1982, she was NBC News White House correspondent, and from 1982 to 1983, chief Washington correspondent for the *Today Show*. She is the author of *This Is Judy Woodruff at the White House* (1982), a founding cochair of the International Women's Media Foundation, and a member of the board of advisers for the John S. Knight Journalism Fellowships at Stanford University and the Freedom Forum First Amendment Center. She is a graduate and trustee of Duke University.

Women, Work, and Family

JUDY WOODRUFF

WHEN THE WOMEN'S MOVEMENT revived a quarter century ago, I was newly graduated from Duke University and just starting my career. Today's college graduates are entering a world that is more far-reaching than anything their parents or I envisioned a generation ago. When we thought about being affected by a faraway place, it was Atlanta or—really far away—New York City. Today's equivalent is Bombay or São Paulo; Americans wake up in the morning to news of the Tokyo stock exchange.

Twenty-five years ago, we used typewriters to write our stories and rewrote them the same way. Computers were so big they filled entire rooms. Twenty-five years ago no woman, including me, could dream about a seat on the U.S. Supreme Court. But we did have dreams. I dreamed of becoming a television journalist.

EARLY ROLE MODELS

My awkward adolescent years were spent in Augusta, Georgia. My family moved there in 1959 when the Army transferred my father from Taiwan to Fort Gordon. After college, I moved to Atlanta, where I worked for eight years. I began as a secretary in the newsroom of a local television station, progressing to local reporter and news anchor and then to roving Southeast-based correspondent for NBC News. Eventually I covered the presidential campaign of a little-known former governor of Georgia. I then left Atlanta in 1977 to cover President Carter for NBC at the White House, and I have been in Washington ever since.

Members of my generation had women role models as we grew up, but they weren't always visible. I can count on one hand the number of women I had even heard of in my field when I decided to go into television journalism: Barbara Walters, Cassie Mackin, and Pauline Frederick. At the same time, I often remember the strong women who made the deepest impressions on me during my growing-up years in Augusta. Those women—who got the most work out of me, who gave me values that remain with me today—(aside from my mother who did *all* these things) were teachers.

I have not forgotten my junior high school English teacher, who gave me a true appreciation of Shakespeare; my just-out-of-college math teacher, who stays in touch with me to this day; and my high school biology teacher, who taught me to have high expectations of myself, even when I squirmed at dissecting a frog. Nor can I forget the many selfless women I met while doing volunteer work at the local Veterans' Administration hospital. It is little-recognized women like these who, in a deeply positive way, influenced my life and the lives of many other women. For all the reputation the South has as a place where women are seen and not heard, where they expect gentlemen to open doors for them and treat them with deference (but not listen to their opinions), I have consistently met women who defy that stereotype. Working in Atlanta, I got to know women who were tireless champions of the needs of minorities, and many women working at the grass-roots on political and community issues.

WOMEN'S GREATER INVOLVEMENT IN POLITICS

What *was* scarce then and what has improved so much since the early 1970s is the involvement of women in elected public office. By 1995, seventy-five years after American women won the right to vote, a record number of women were serving in the U.S. Congress. In 1992, more women ran as major party candidates for Congress than ever before; the number of women in the House of Representatives climbed from twenty-eight to an all-time high of forty-seven. Following the 1994 election, the number of women in the Senate reached a record of eight, or 8 percent—still a tiny portion of the total one hundred members, but a four-fold increase since 1992. By 1995, women held more than 20 percent of state legislative seats; in 1969, only 4 percent of all state legislators were women. Moreover, by 1995, a record 26 percent of all statewide offices were held by women. At the municipal and county level, the number of women officeholders more than tripled in the past twenty years.

Starting with the election cycle of 1992, women congressional candidates raised record amounts of campaign money—and more *women* gave to women than ever before. It is no secret that women traditionally have had a harder time than men raising money for political campaigns. Paradoxically, money, the "mother's milk" of politics, didn't flow in abundance to women until the final years of the twentieth century. The fact that voters are now contributing to women—and that women are writing checks more freely—is good news for women candidates in the future.

When it comes to electing women to public office, numbers matter of course. But what matters even more is what will these women do? The evidence is that things will change. That already was starting to happen when Anita Hill testified at the Senate confirmation hearings of Supreme Court Justice Clarence Thomas. No matter whether one believes his side of the story or hers, there is no denying that a collective wave of anger swept through American women in the fall of 1991, anger that spilled over into the elections of 1992. It reflected a profound feeling that the issues of sexual harassment and discrimination in the workplace needed to be brought out into the open.

None of this means that all double standards have been erased. We should not forget that in 1993 several of President Clinton's women nominees were dropped from consideration at least in part because it was discovered that they had not paid social security taxes for domestic workers providing child care, when men with children were barely asked the question. That tells us a lot about how women are perceived, even when they are under consideration for one of the top jobs in government.

Nevertheless, times are changing, particularly with respect to issues that disproportionately affect women and their children. The newcomers to the corridors of power are bringing a fresh, woman's perspective to many issues that have not had one before. As usual, much of what really matters has begun to happen on the state and local level.

In New Hampshire, for example, it was women politicians who led the effort requiring insurers to cover bone-marrow transplants for breast cancer victims. In Maine, a bipartisan group of women legislators successfully pushed for a law permitting nurse practitioners to practice in rural areas without the supervision of doctors. In Arizona, women legislators persuaded their colleagues to pass legislation allowing juries to hear about a history of household domestic violence in certain cases. And women politicians in several states forced insurance companies to permit longer hospital stays for mothers and their newborn babies.

Overall, what we have seen about women in politics is that in the 1990s, after years of exclusion from the old boys' network, women *profited* from that exclusion as candidates for public office. Voters wanted change, and not many women could be accused of being part of the status quo. So their outsider's status, so painful for so long, finally became an asset. However, voters yearning for a fresh face after every election also unseated newly elected women incumbents. For many years, incumbency was the biggest hurdle women candidates had to overcome; once women themselves became incumbents, we expected them to stay a while. It is too early to tell, however, whether or not the rules suddenly changed just as women candidates figured out how to play them to their advantage.

More women also are now serving in important appointed executive branch positions in the federal government. I have no doubt that my daughter and other people's daughters will think more broadly about their life options after they look up and see a woman attorney general or head of the Office of Management and Budget discussing important matters on the television news. When we look outside government, we see women reaching pinnacles across the board, in such positions as college presidents and heads of nonprofit organizations. But—and this is a big *but*—the picture is spotty. In business, women have made inroads into middle management but are having a harder time reaching the top. In my field of journalism, women news editors and senior managers are still few and far between, even as women broadcasting on the air proliferate.

Over the past twenty years or so, we have become a much better and more productive society because we have twice as many women doctors, three times as many women economists, and more than four times as many women lawyers and judges. Women also now make up 57 percent of all bartenders, compared to only 27 percent two decades ago, though I'm not sure that's the sort of advance envisioned by Susan B. Anthony, the great suffragist and crusader for temperance!

THE IMPORTANCE OF FAMILY

All this progress, of course, has prompted numerous news stories about the unprecedented rise in the number of mothers who work outside the home. There are many women, like me, who seek professional and personal fulfillment through a career. But there are many more who have been forced to get a paying job because their families need their incomes.

One of the first questions many young women ask me—and, encouragingly more and more men, too—is, "How hard is it to combine career and family?" That this question is raised at all is testament to the women's movement, to which all Americans—male as well as female—owe a huge debt. I know we will never go back to the days of Ozzie and Harriet, when women didn't have the opportunities they have today. What I dream about instead is a day in the future when men and women alike have options: options to stay home, to work away from home, or to combine the two. I know from my own experience that family and career can be combined. At the same time, I know from experience that it is not easy.

I still laugh about that week when I broke up a trip to Ohio, where I was covering the president of the United States, to fly home for a fifth-grade sleep over. I spent the night on the floor of a school gym, where we looked at the stars through a telescope, then I got up early the next morning, flew back to Ohio, and finished my reporting. I am lucky to have a great job. But I don't spend weekends thinking about Newt Gingrich or Bill Clinton or capital gains tax rates or even North Korea's nuclear capability. I worry about balancing soccer games and baseball practices with school picnics and sleep overs. Al Hunt, my husband, and I have three children, and there is one constant in our lives: we are always tired!

It's a tough, constant struggle. Almost every day, I worry—like most other mothers who work outside the home—whether I am striking the proper balance and what the long-lasting effects of my choice will be on my children. I feel guilty on those occasions when I miss a school play or a soccer game or get home too late to help with homework (our society's expectations of mothers have left a deep impression on me). But I believe I am a better mother and wife because I am fulfilled at work, and I know that I am a better journalist because of the joys of my family.

Like anything worthwhile, combining work and family requires real commitment. I often tell young people this: when you dream about the impressive goals you will achieve, dream just as hard about your family. And if you choose to become a full-time homemaker and care-giver, know what an honorable choice you have made.

We must remember that whatever choices women and men make, there are clear correlations between family structure and poverty, crime, and academic success. We must remember that parents today spend, overall, 40 percent less time with their children than parents did in 1965. Indeed, America at the end of the twentieth century is faced with a crisis of family. It is a crisis that affects every woman and man in this democracy because it tears at the fabric of the greatness of this country. The breakdown may be more severely felt by lower socio-economic groups, but it affects middle-class and well-to-do families as well.

We have all heard the statistics. In lower-, middle-, and upper-income families, cases of child abuse and child neglect have soared. Today, not only are more and more children born out of wedlock, more children are also born into two-parent families affected by divorce. The divorce rate has doubled over the past quarter century. Senator Daniel Patrick Moynihan was bitterly assailed a few decades ago for writing that at the center of what he called America's "tangle of pathology" is the weakness of the family. Now, there is no disputing the profound effects of family breakdown. More than one-fifth of American children under eighteen live in poverty. But only about 10 percent of children in two-parent households are poor, compared to more than half of children in female-headed households. Despite that, some of the most courageous and remarkable people in America are single parents who are overcoming enormous adversities to give their children love, support, and discipline. The history of this nation, indeed, is built upon a people who have overcome the odds.

But while America remains the envy of the world in economics, higher education, and most other competitive barometers, it certainly is not the envy of the world in terms of family stability and sense of individual responsibility—the core relationships and values that define us as a people.

On the one hand, liberals have mistakenly associated concerns about a breakdown in family values as somehow demeaning to the poor or even a mild form of racism. But it is the poor, and especially the minority poor, who are most frequently the victims; not to face up to this is to relegate them to another generation of hopelessness. Too many conservatives, on the other hand, have long argued that people have to take care of themselves, that all government does is make the problems worse.

Without question, many examples of government inefficiency and indifference exist. But that is not the whole story. In 1965, one-third of America's elderly lived in poverty; today only 12 percent are poor, primarily because of Medicare, Supplemental Security Income, and other government programs. Likewise, Head Start and the federal Women, Infants, and Children program should not be viewed as just more government spending; they are investments in children and families that demonstrably work.

Government at all levels has a role to play. So do each of us. Indeed, those of us in a position to make a difference bear a special responsibility. In ways large and small, we can make a difference. That is, if we care, if we have a sense of indignation, if we insist that certain conditions are unacceptable in this greatest nation on earth.

In the context of making a difference, we must not let a focus on personal success overshadow the fundamental importance of family, both our individual families and the families formed by our communities. Each of us must expect better of our public and private sectors. We must hold politicians' feet to the fire. We must demand that employers, especially major companies, follow the example of firms that already place an emphasis on family, such as Johnson & Johnson, Aetna, Corning, and IBM.

None of us can predict the future. But there always will be room for hard-working, creative people who very much want to make a contribution. What is most important is that each of us singles out the area she wants to contribute to, the needy spot in which to pour her passion, and works just as hard as she can in that area. You may barely make ends meet doing this. But at the end of most days, you will feel fulfilled, feel that you are making a contribution, and you will not be consumed with worry about how much more you wish you were earning.

Each of us can try to make a difference in a child's life. We can take time to help a young less fortunate child in a single-parent or nonparent home. We can spend just two hours a week with that boy or girl, only a little more than 1 percent of our time. Some of us may be able to do a lot more; all of us should be able to at least do this.

As Americans, we have so much to be grateful for. We live in the freest country on earth. As women, we have come a very long way; we have opportunities few of us ever dreamed of just ten, fifteen, or twenty-five years ago. And we are vastly enriched by those women who came before us: who blazed trails, who faced down critics, who raised children, who spoke up for what they believed in, who were not always visible. They made a difference.

ESTHER PETERSON was special assistant to the president for consumer affairs (1964–1967 and 1977–1980), director of the Women's Bureau of the U.S. Department of Labor (1961–1964), and assistant secretary of labor for labor standards (1961–1969). She taught in Utah and Boston and at the Bryn Mawr Summer School for Women Workers in Industry (1932–1939) before becoming assistant director of education (1939–1944) and then Washington legislative representative for the Amalgamated Clothing Workers of America (1945–1948) and for the AFL-CIO (1958–1961). She is a former president of the National Consumers League and board member of Common Cause. She holds an A.B. degree from Brigham Young University and an M.A. degree from Columbia Teachers College. In 1981, she was awarded the Presidential Medal of Freedom.

Do What Is Right

ESTHER PETERSON

*I*N THE EARLY 1930S, during the Great Depression, I learned about injustice firsthand. At the time, I was a teacher during the day at an elite school for upper-income children. In the evenings, I worked as a YWCA volunteer, teaching women factory workers gymnastics and tap dancing. One evening, however, the women didn't come to class. I decided to find the reason why.

I discovered that the women were on strike. They worked making housedresses at a piecework rate of $1.32 per dozen. The factory owners had redesigned the pockets on the dresses from a square to a heart shape. It took longer to make the dresses, and so the women earned less money. When the company refused to increase wages to compensate for the harder work they were asked to perform, the women went on what they termed "the heartbreak strike."

This was still the sweatshop period in America. The situation of the women workers made me furious. I soon became involved in the heartbreak strike. When police on horseback escorted strikebreakers through the picket line, I recruited some of the mothers of my well-to-do daytime students who, dressed in expensive coats, walked into the crowd. The mounted police didn't dare charge into them. That was when I discovered it helps to have important people standing by your side if you want to get things done.

The heartbreak strike was a turning point for me. It taught me hard lessons. I learned that the poverty of one group was making another wealthy. I knew that fathers of the children I taught during the day were exploiting garment workers I taught at night. Chauffeurs delivered the factory owners' children to school in the morning, yet the owners claimed they could not afford to pay their employees a living wage. In the end, the International Ladies Garment Workers Union helped the women win higher wages. That experience got me started as an organizer and reformer. I also learned that one person cannot do everything alone; it is critical that people work together for a cause.

Next I taught in a wonderful educational project, the Bryn Mawr Summer School for Women Workers in Industry. Women factory workers came to the college for courses taught by top university scholars; they also listened to such prominent visiting lecturers as Eleanor Roosevelt and Margaret Sanger. The students studied everything from economics to poetry and took part in sports and dramatic productions. We built courses around the women's lives and taught the principles of democracy and citizen participation. In 1938, however, the school closed; its financing disappeared when several students were accused of participating in a strike. Some of the summer school students returned to the factories; others, however, had learned enough about social structure in America to become union organizers, social workers, and teachers.

I grew up in a Mormon family on the frontier in Utah. I was raised to believe that whatever you do should be for the good; that you must take responsibility for your own actions and be sure you are not hurting anyone else. A traditional hymn we used to sing in church is central to my life: "Do what is right; let the consequence follow."

When I became a friend and colleague of Eleanor Roosevelt, she impressed me with her concern for people who are left out and her willingness to reach out to the less fortunate. She wanted to learn about things firsthand, and so she would visit ordinary people and see how they lived. A woman of great modesty, Eleanor Roosevelt often said that she would not speak about an issue unless she had seen it or experienced it herself.

Long before her husband became president, Eleanor Roosevelt's leadership pointed the way for women to be respected as serious players in politics. She helped get us past the notion that women had no role in politics other than to lick envelopes and stick on stamps. The attitude that women's time, ideas, and leadership were not valuable had always bothered me. When President Kennedy appointed me as assistant secretary of labor and director of the Women's Bureau in 1961, my job was to improve the status of women, especially working women. We sought legislation mandating equal pay for equal work, and President Kennedy created the President's Commission on the Status of Women.

Today women still earn less than men, but in the early 1960s, an equal pay law did not exist, and structural barriers also accounted for wage disparities. Classified employment ads were divided into "men wanted" and "women wanted" categories; employers paid "women's wages" and "men's wages."

Although many organizations began working for an equal pay law at the end of World War II, it was not until 1963 that it became law, following the recommendation of the President's Commission on the Status of Women. The Equal Pay Act not only required equal pay for equal work, it also set a precedent for government involvement in private-sector practices that discriminated against women. It eliminated the structural barriers to equal pay and allowed women to sue for wage comparability and back pay. Eleanor Roosevelt chaired the commission, which consisted of fifteen women and eleven men who were leaders in labor unions, women's organizations, and government, including a number of cabinet secretaries. More than one hundred other individuals, women and men, were involved in the commission's work as members of its subcommittees.

The commission's final report, presented to President Kennedy in October 1963, enumerated the pervasiveness of inequality for women in the United States. Entitled *American Women*, it documented discriminatory practices under the law and in the workplace and high-lighted the lack of social services such as child care for working women. In addition to equal pay, the commission sought coverage under the Fair Labor Standards Act of occupations generally filled by women, oc-cupations up to then exempted from wage and hours laws. Rather than immediately seeking an equal rights amendment to the U.S. Constitu-tion, the commission called first for a series of lawsuits to test whether the U.S. Supreme Court would conclude that the 5th and 14th Amend-ment guarantees applied to women as equals under the law.

To implement the commission's report, President Kennedy issued a presidential order requiring the civil service not to discriminate on the basis of sex. He appointed a Citizens' Advisory Council on the Status of Women and an Interdepartmental Commission on the Status of Women made up of cabinet officials. President Johnson carried out what President Kennedy started. In 1964, he signed the landmark Civil Rights Act, which includes Title VII, outlawing discrimination on the basis of race or sex in employment.

The commission's report not only served as an agenda for national reform but also activated many local women's organizations. Com-missions for women were formed in most of the states, creating a net-work of women who shared information and ideas for change. At the grassroots, the women's movement was beginning a vigorous revival.

Much has changed since then. Growing numbers of American women have made a genuine mark on this nation by showing that women can and do contribute equally with men in all aspects of life. Women in elective and appointive positions have influenced a broad range of issues that had been neglected in a male-dominated society. The problems of working women, child care and health care concerns, and family assistance needs were largely ignored until women began making them priorities.

But there is still so much left to do. Our lists are filled with unfin-ished business in health, housing, and education. Moreover, we have not fully learned how to provide meaningful assistance to persons with many kinds of needs, not just physical needs.

The functioning of American democracy and the fulfillment of the democratic principle have benefited from increasing participation by women. If our system did not have women's full participation, it would be misleading to call it democratic. But we women have not made as great a difference as we could because we have not sufficiently exercised the privileges that we already have. With wider participation and better informed participants, our political effectiveness can be much improved.

The right of women to vote has moved us toward fulfillment of our democratic society, toward the concept that we *all* count. But we still need to convince all individuals that they count. Moreover, we need to convince them that they count *negatively* when they do not participate. We must inspire more women to get involved and understand that they *can* and do make a difference.

We all need to feel important in this democracy and to understand that we are needed. We can start with small steps: write a letter, make a phone call. Complain, yes—but go ahead and also *do* something. We must never forget that it is involving other people in the issues we care about that adds up to political effectiveness and success.

Democracy means that one can speak up—be heard, be respected, have one's voice count. It means more fairness to all as we work for a common purpose, each person sacrificing a little for the good of everyone. Democracy means accepting decisions arrived at through common beliefs and understandings, decisions in which my voice and your voice are heard. This process requires compromise, but as Eleanor Roosevelt used to remind me: "Compromise, but always compromise upward!"

I hope my granddaughters will remember me for trying to achieve wider political participation for all women; especially low-income people—the people usually left out. I want my grandchildren to treasure a principle that has stayed with me since childhood and is expressed in the old Mormon hymn that says: "Have I done any good today? Have I helped anyone in need? If not, I have failed indeed."

And I still sing that other hymn from my youth: "Do what is right; let the consequence follow."

ANNE FIROR SCOTT is W.K. Boyd Professor of History emerita at Duke University. Her most recent books include *Making the Invisible Woman Visible* (1984), *Natural Allies: Women's Associations in American History* (1991), and *Unheard Voices* (1993). Her pathbreaking *The Southern Lady* (1970) was reissued in a 25th anniversary edition with a new afterword in 1995. She was president of the Organization of American Historians (1983–1984) and the Southern Historical Association (1988–1989); served on the boards of the Woodrow Wilson International Center for Scholars, Carnegie Corporation, and Schlesinger Library; and chaired the North Carolina Governor's Commission on the Status of Women (1963–1964). She earned her A.B. degree from the University of Georgia, M.A. degree from Northwestern University, and Ph.D. degree from Radcliffe College.

My Life with
the League of
Women Voters

ANNE FIROR SCOTT

MY HISTORY AND THAT of the League of Women Voters coin-
cided during the years from 1944 to 1947. Looking back, I see
the experience as tremendously educational, one that—unbeknownst
to me at the time—was laying the foundation for what would become
an important part of my later scholarly career.

My first encounter with the league came on a hot August day in
1944 when its national president Anna Lord Strauss and vice president
Kathryn Stone, with what I would learn to respect as typical league fru-
gality, took me to lunch at the YWCA cafeteria. I believe my lunch cost
ninety cents.

Earlier that year, a revolution had taken place at the national league
convention. Delegates voted to abolish the structure that the league

inherited from its predecessor organization, the National American Woman Suffrage Association. From a federation of state affiliates, the League of Women Voters had transformed itself into an organization based upon individual members. Moreover, for the first time since the league's founding in 1920, the 1944 convention had rejected the slate of officers recommended by the nominating committee and had elected a president and board from the floor. Chosen to lead the organization through a period of profound change, Anna Strauss, like the League of Women Voters itself, had her roots in woman suffrage. She was the great-granddaughter of abolitionist and suffragist Lucretia Coffin Mott and had been a leader in the League of Women Voters of New York.

Following the 1944 convention, two longtime staff members, women with Ph.D. degrees and lots of experience, resigned to take better paying jobs in the war-stressed Department of State. Anna Strauss, faced with the need to rebuild her staff at a time when the demand for qualified people was higher than it had ever been, solved the problem by finding young people whom she could train. As a result, the program staff was made up of Margaret Terry, a recent Stanford graduate; Zelia Ruebhausen, a Vassar graduate; and me—three years out of the University of Georgia and the possessor of a recent master's degree in international relations from Northwestern University. It was sink or swim as we began writing for *Trends* (ancestor of the league's *National Voter*) and producing numerous pamphlets for the use of local leagues. We also took our share of field trips.

Our small office stretched along one corridor in a building near the White House on Jackson Place. The staff numbered roughly a dozen, and everybody did some of everything, though some had special responsibilities for working with Congress, for keeping the budget, and for organizing new leagues.

In the 1940s, Carrie Chapman Catt was still writing often to Anna Strauss, and several of the most important woman suffrage leaders were still active in the league: Maud Wood Park, in Maine; Katherine

Ludington, in Connecticut; and Mary Foulke Morrisson, also in Connecticut. They were, one and all, extraordinarily impressive women: intelligent, highly educated (often by their own efforts), and beautiful.

Maud Wood Park, the league's first national president (from 1920 to 1924), brought to the organization political acumen and diplomatic skills of a high order. Mary Foulke Morrisson, a longtime social reformer, was one of Carrie Chapman Catt's lieutenants and a founder of the league. Katherine Ludington, the league's national treasurer from 1922 to 1927, was especially interested in foreign policy. She did her best to train me up in the way I should go. She must have been in her seventies; I was twenty-three. Now that I am in my seventies and occasionally grow impatient with the twenty-somethings, I remember the generosity and care these women exerted and try to emulate them.

We were engaged in developing community discussions on major issues: the plans for a United Nations, the plans for a Missouri Valley Authority, the Bretton Woods meeting on international trade. With a little help from an artistically talented friend, I managed to produce something called *The Story of Dumbarton Oaks,* which was distributed by local leagues all over the country to build public support for the founding of the United Nations. To our surprise, over 100,000 copies were sold in only a few weeks.

From time to time, we were sent to visit the field. I am sure Anna Strauss thought it important to keep league national staff close to the real world that local league presidents faced, making sure that when we came to write our articles and pamphlets we had the nature of our audience clearly in mind. It was wonderful training. I learned to lead discussions. I learned how women's voluntary associations had developed to exercise political influence. Above all, I learned that women could do almost anything they set their minds to.

In 1947, I left to get married and to begin work on a Ph.D. in history at Harvard. In 1951, back in Washington with a new baby, I thought my professional life was over for awhile. But Percy Maxim Lee, then national president of the league, thought otherwise. She devised a part-time job, and soon I was back at work, first as the league's congressional representative and then as editor of the *National Voter*. Field trips were fewer but still fascinating. I was, for example, sent to Atlanta in 1952, where the league was already preparing for what would become the landmark 1954 case *Brown* v. *Topeka Board of Education*. I wish I had a tape of that meeting!

In 1953, the Scotts left Washington for good, but for a few years, first in New Hampshire and then in Pennsylvania and finally in Chapel Hill, North Carolina, I was on the other side of the fence as a local league member. I listened with interest to all the things my colleagues had to say about "national"—not always complimentary things; though on the whole, I believe the national organization was respected. My co-worker Zelia Ruebhausen also left the league staff and became an active volunteer. Her long interest and expertise in foreign policy served her well: from 1945 to 1960, she was the first official League of Women Voters observer at the United Nations. Margaret Terry developed a distinguished career in school counseling.

Years went by. I became a historian, my interest turned to women's history, and before long, I was writing about the part women's voluntary associations had played in the forming of American society—first in *The Southern Lady* (1970), then in many articles, and finally in *Natural Allies* (1992). It all began in that little office on Jackson Place.

The League of Women Voters, like almost everything else in American society, has changed remarkably since the 1950s. I would not today be able to find my way around the national office. The national president can operate with a computer no matter where she lives—I wonder what Anna Strauss would make of that if she could return? The size and complexity of the staff, the operation of the board, and the nature of the publications are all different. It startles me to recall that when I joined the staff in 1944, the organization was only twenty-four years old and so was woman suffrage. Now more than forty years have gone by since I left. No wonder things are different.

CORINNE C. "LINDY" BOGGS was U.S. Representative from Louisiana's Second District (1973–1991). The first woman to represent Louisiana in the U.S. House of Representatives, she is the first to chair a major party convention (1976), to serve as regent of the Smithsonian Institute, and to receive the Distinguished and Outstanding Alumni Award of Tulane University (1985) and the Congressional Award of the Veterans of Foreign Wars (1986). She is a graduate of Sophie Newcomb College at Tulane University and holds several honorary doctorates. To "remember the ladies" and Representative Boggs, Congress in 1991 rededicated the historic room in the U.S. Capitol building where Abigail Adams's son, John Quincy Adams, died. It is now the "Lindy Claiborne Boggs Congresswoman's Reading Room."

Keepers of the Culture

CORINNE C. "LINDY" BOGGS

O N THE 200TH ANNIVERSARY of the signing of the United States
Constitution, I was selected by my colleagues in the Congress
to preside over a reenactment of the signing of the Connecticut Compromise. It was the Connecticut Compromise that provided for the legislative branch of the federal government two senators from each state
regardless of its size and representatives proportionate in number to the
size of each state's population.

As I left Constitution Hall, I was asked by an awestruck woman,
"How did it feel to sit in George Washington's chair?" My mind and
heart raced back two hundred years to Benjamin Franklin's emergence
from the same building after the long hot battle that finally produced
a Constitution that could be signed. He was met by a woman who in-
quired, "Dr. Franklin, what kind of government have you given us, a

monarchy, or a republic?" Franklin replied, "A republic, madam, if you can keep it."

I was struck by the realization that the women of the United States have indeed kept our republic with fervor and intelligence and dedicated service throughout the wars, the near wars, the plagues, the depressions, the agricultural age, the industrial age, the scientific and technological age, and the beginning of the information age.

To commemorate the passage of woman suffrage, the National Archives launched a special project in 1994, entitled *Our Mothers Before Us: Women and Democracy, 1789–1920,* which focuses on women's civic contributions before they had the right to vote. It highlights women's involvement in the abolition of slavery; the Civil War and the Reconstruction; the Western expansion (in which the women who migrated confronted the challenge of building new communities and institutions and petitioned Congress on the issues of statehood, Native American rights, and suffrage); the temperance movement; the Progressive Era's social and political reforms in the areas of education, labor, food and drug purity, maternal and infant health, and antilynching legislation; and of course, woman suffrage, which finally was ratified in a Constitutional amendment after a lengthy and passionate national campaign by countless heroic women and men.

My father's eldest sister, Celeste Claiborne Carruth, was a leader of the woman suffrage movement in Louisiana, which had been plagued with the difficulties of competing groups and differences of opinions on states' rights and national prerogatives. The patience and the authority of the National American Woman Suffrage Association (NAWSA) (whose national convention had been held in New Orleans in 1903) was tested by similar and additional controversies that had arisen among many women's groups in the various states. The women throughout all the states were blessed by the resolution of these tensions when the NAWSA amended its constitution in 1919 to include a League of Women Voters to "increase the effectiveness of women's votes in furthering better government."

My entire life has been directly influenced by the ratification of woman suffrage. I was four years old when the 19th Amendment was ratified, and at the time I was old enough to vote, I became the woman's precinct captain of the fifth precinct of the twelfth ward in the City of New Orleans. In Louisiana, the success of the state's vote for woman suffrage had been thwarted by the powerful New Orleans mayor Martin Behrman and his so-called ring. Finally, in 1938, eighteen years after woman suffrage was won, the women of New Orleans organized a gallant political movement that cooperated with a statewide reform organization to replace corrupt government officials with the reform candidates they supported. Their victory has engaged me in political activities all the days of my life.

Two years later, my husband, Hale Boggs, was elected to the 77th Congress, and our two babies and I accompanied him to Washington. There I met Representative Jeannette Rankin of Montana, who had been elected to Congress the year I was born. (The pioneer states had included woman suffrage in their state constitutions.) She had voted against U.S. participation in World War I and was not returned to Congress. As fate would have it, she was reelected to Congress in time to vote against our entry into World War II and again suffered a loss in the following election. I was fortunate, as were the other congressional wives and the women members of Congress, to experience her bright mind, her vast energy, and her indomitable spirit.

Throughout the years of World War II, when the women of America assumed responsibilities imposed upon them, they performed with valor and effectiveness. The women actively engaged in war—the WACs, the WAVEs, the WASPs, the women in the Nurses Corps—and the women civilians who supported the war effort formed the basis of the strong and unrelenting movement for women's rights. As their foremothers had done, they pressed also for the rights of all persons and for the care of the children, the aged, the displaced, the ill, and the disadvantaged. The Vietnam War was both a distraction and a solidifier to their movement.

Despite their gains and valiant determination, the women of the United States have not been successful in their push to ratify the Equal

Rights Amendment. However, one by one, sometimes painfully, most of the rights that would have been guaranteed by the ERA have been passed separately by succeeding Congresses.

When my husband disappeared in 1972 while campaigning for Congressman Nick Begich in Alaska, I ran and was elected to his seat in the House of Representatives. I was the first woman from Louisiana to serve in that capacity. As does every congresswoman, I became a surrogate member for many women who were not represented by a woman. The problems and dreams and solid suggestions for effective change were presented to congresswomen individually, but we felt we could be more effective working as a group. And so the Congresswoman's Caucus was established. Soon the Caucus formed a research organization, the Women's Research and Educational Institute. From these combined resources of political power and solid information emanated much of the legislation establishing equal opportunity, equal credit, equal education in sciences and mathematics, equal representation in health research and health care, and equal opportunities in sports and athletic training.

Throughout my husband's service and mine, I have been gratified by the blessings that the 19th Amendment has conferred upon our children and grandchildren, and especially our daughters and granddaughters. Our daughter Barbara Sigmund, who died of cancer in 1991, was an accomplished politician. She first was elected a Mercer County, New Jersey, "chosen freeholder" and then mayor of Princeton. Our daughter Cokie Roberts, a congressional correspondent for ABC News and National Public Radio, has given us great pride. So have our granddaughters Elizabeth Davidsen, who has served with the United Nations and the Inter American Development Bank, and Rebecca Roberts, who is associated with a political public relations firm in Philadelphia, that city where Benjamin Franklin first enlisted the help of the women to keep our republic.

As I watch my three-year-old great-granddaughter Caroline wrest her space shuttle toy from my four-year-old great-grandson Andrew's grasp, I feel confident that the United States will continue to produce highly competent women scientists, women astronauts, and women activists who will sustain a government geared to their advancement in their chosen fields and to the protection of their personal rights.

As we enter the first century of the next millennium, my advice to all my grandchildren and great-grandchildren of both sexes includes that they dream great dreams, write serious tomes and frivolous poems, devise new laws and rules and procedures pertinent to new discoveries and opportunities and situations, and soar to the heights of the political, academic, religious, and cultural worlds. In the doing, I would admonish them not to neglect the chores of democracy and the fundamental obligations of American women as the keepers of the culture, as well as the republic, for the next generation.

One legacy of my generation to my daughters' generation is that my generation walked that path, enabling the following generation to grow up seeing it more clearly.

My childhood was lived in a small town in Kansas. I knew somehow that I could and would be somebody, but there was little in my surroundings that encouraged that belief. Every middle-class person there lived a similar story. There were two parents in every home. The father earned the money, and the mother, who took care of the house and children, spent it. The mother played bridge, and the father handled politics, debating issues with his male friends and colleagues in their male clubs: the Knights of Columbus, the chamber of commerce, the American Legion, and in Kansas, the Knife and Fork Club. Before entering the voting booth, husbands would softly remind wives, "If you do not vote as I do, you will cancel my vote." These good folks of the plains, second- and third-generation Americans, raised their children in their own images: "One day, my son will own my shoe store, and my daughter will marry well."

Politics was my father's passion, and I shared it. I loved going around the state and being hailed as my father's daughter, and my father loved it, too. But his tune changed when I told him I wanted to become a lawyer, like him: "Why would you want to do that? The only woman lawyer I know is a librarian in Denver. How about being a schoolteacher or a social worker? Something to fall back on if you need it."

So I, Barbara Joan Davis, earned a master of social work degree and became a social worker. But I left Kansas and even Denver behind. What moved me, a daughter of those good plains folk, to want to be independent? To make a difference? To change the world? From the safe vantage of today, I can see that boredom and rebellion against my parents pushed me but that the great promise of democracy, implicit in the hundreds of books I read, pulled me out of Kansas. It never once occurred to me that I could not, with wit, education, and hard work, become what I wanted to be. Whatever that was!

It was not as easy as I thought it would be. There was no career path for a woman, and no one to help me develop one. Instead, I traveled an obstacle course: turn left, go right, veer back, jump! Everywhere I met the ingrained belief in others—but never in me or in the female friends I chose—that women were not as capable as men. But I jumped with gusto on every opportunity. I jumped from Florida to New York to Georgia. I went from social worker to clinic director to entrepreneur to businesswoman to community leader. I began to see specific things I wanted to change. Then my path became clearer: if I believed new laws were needed, I either had to be elected to write them, or I had to work for the election of people who believed as I did.

I became a civic leader, heading a group responsible for the passage of the first land-use planning law in the South and the creation of one of the country's first Urban National Recreation Areas. I was offered and accepted appointments to Atlanta and Georgia public-sector boards and commissions.

Then came a huge stroke of luck. Jimmy Carter, the visionary, intelligent, and kind governor of my state, whom I revered because of his enlightened policies in the still semisegregated South, decided to run for president. I was appointed deputy political director of his primary campaign, and he won. I became the deputy director of his presidential campaign and his postelection transition team, and then deputy administrator of the U.S. Environmental Protection Agency, where I could affect environmental policy across the nation and even internationally.

Now I am a banker whose clientele is primarily public interest organizations, small businesses and women- and minority-owned businesses, a reflection of all my values and my abiding friendships.

My bank's business is clearly not typical bank business, and the bank name declares its special mission. Adams National Bank is named for Abigail Smith Adams, wife of this nation's second president and mother of its sixth, and surely one of our first supporters of women's rights. As early as the drafting of the Declaration of Independence, she was lobbying her husband for woman suffrage. We women, she wrote in a letter to him, "will not hold ourselves bound by any laws in which we have no voice, or representation."

Adams National Bank is a living monument to the visionary women on whose shoulders we stand and a proud statement of women's exploding economic achievements today. Over the bank's seventeen-year history, its loans to women entrepreneurs have fostered the development of hundreds of new and expanding businesses and thousands of new jobs.

I trace my success directly to woman suffrage, for the path I walked was the democratic political process. Through the political process and only through the political process can one individual work for public policy changes that will benefit many people and endure into the future. In a country where everything is new, the inclusion of American women in our democracy is especially new. We women are only just beginning to explore our potential for political and economic power. The two world wars gave us our first taste of the men's work world. Affirmative action has encouraged men who would not otherwise have thought of doing so to give us a job, a promotion, a contract. But we must take all these threads of opportunity and weave the tapestry of power ourselves.

In the early 1960s, original thinkers like Betty Friedan spoke for many of us and gave us permission to strive for equality and achievement without suffering guilt. Other women leaders arose, and many of us joined demonstrations for women's rights, an end to the Vietnam War, and the enforcement of civil rights for minorities. But there has been no focal point for women to rally around in order to achieve true power. I have always believed we should start with the electoral process, and our progress in this area has been slow but steady.

In 1976, as deputy director of the Carter-Mondale campaign, I began to help develop women's electoral power base. Those of us who were the women leaders in the campaign created a campaign division called Fifty-One Point Three, after the percentage of women in the population. We identified issues we thought were of special interest to women, such as pay equity, equal access to jobs, equal access to credit, and the right to choose an abortion, and got them included in the Democratic platform. We pushed successfully for more women at the top levels of the campaign and soon found that the word was "trickling down"—women started appearing in prominent campaign roles at the regional and local levels, too.

I traveled all over the country, with Jimmy Carter and alone, and met with women everywhere, urging them to coalesce around the issues. Often meetings took place right at the airport, and I would move on immediately to the next city. We set up our Women's Talent Bank, collecting résumés from across the country so we would be ready to name qualified women available for each top administration position. No one on our watch would ever be able to say there were no "qualified women" available for any job. At last, the ball was rolling. This was the first all-out well-organized effort in American politics to mobilize the women's vote as a bloc in order to influence the machinery of democracy. While we were only moderately successful, we certainly helped elect a compassionate president who did not oppose a woman's right to choose an abortion and who was an ambassador for human rights at home and around the world.

Despite our having had superior numbers in the population and among registered voters before this time, 1980 was the first election year in which women actually voted in higher numbers than men. That trend has continued. Women are now 58 percent of the registered voters and could swing any election in which the nature of the debate motivated them to come to the polls. We could change America socially and economically overnight—if we could be motivated to vote together, to concentrate on what connects us rather than what divides us.

Women have long known from their daily experiences what connects them to other women. We know from our conversations with friends, with co-workers, with other women at places of worship and voluntary organizations and children's schools, with store clerks and fellow bus passengers that our overriding concerns are the safety and well-being of our families. We also know that despite the many stressful roles we play, we are buoyed with great pride and satisfaction over our ability to juggle those roles and make ever increasing contributions toward the quality of life of our families and our communities.

Women's Voices, a serious poll that confirms this anecdotal lore, was released in 1992 by the Ms. Foundation for Women and the Center for Policy Alternatives, which I chair. It proved, first, that women's primary concerns resonate across the lines of race, ethnicity, and socioeconomic class. We all worry about our ability to protect the quality of life for our families, as measured by our having the time to manage our families and our jobs, having good health care for our families including our older parents, and having equality in pay and an end to job discrimination so that we have the means to provide for our families.

Equal pay for equal work is the issue that would move most women to action. Over three-fourths of us want equal pay laws as well as laws to end discrimination in employment and promotion. Almost half of us have experienced a problem with equal pay, either personally or through someone we know. If women would speak together on this issue at the polls, this discrimination would no longer be tolerated.

We must make the men who make the political decisions realize that it is in their interest to end the discrimination. They, after all, are family members and will benefit from the family's improved economic power and the increasing pride felt by the women in their lives.

An interesting insight into the problem of discrimination is that we women have great faith in our democracy's ability to correct it. Fully three-fourths of us want the government to enact antidiscrimination and pay equity laws; among minority women, the number tops 80 percent. Our concern is not a yuppie preoccupation with material things but rather an expression of our frustration at not being able to contribute more. This is a real and a daily struggle. Our unifying desire is for a policy that will allow us to make enough money to make ends meet and to combine with ease and grace our work and family lives.

The second important poll finding reported in *Women's Voices* is that issues like reproductive choice, issues the public regards as "feminist" (read "radical" or "unpopular"), although supported by a large majority of women, are not the top priority for many. Despite the loud public debate on these issues, we are not fooled. We know that economic issues are the top priority, and we know that what we need most is a fair shot at earning our real worth in the job market. Yet we have allowed those opposed to positive change for women, aided and abetted by the media penchant for oversimplification and sensation, to define the issues and make it appear that women's voices are divided in cacophony. In reality, we are united.

From the poll, we also know that women credit the women's movement with increasing their opportunities and heightening people's awareness of inequality. Nearly three-fourths of women believe women's lives have changed for the better as a result of the women's movement. Now women are prepped to move to the next levels of political action. And indeed, we strongly support the idea of women leaders. The tidal wave of support for women running for elected office has not been exaggerated. Nearly three-quarters of the *Women's Voices* participants believe women would be better off today if women held half of all elected offices.

We know that our lives are marked by change and stress but also deep satisfaction. We have one foot firmly planted in home and family and the other firmly planted in the workplace. It is time for us to develop public policies that are based on this reality and not on nostalgia for a mythical past. We must find the means and the incentive to educate ourselves politically, inform the policy discussion, and thus sharpen the public debate to bring about the changes we all want and need. Women are united in a clear policy agenda that easily translates into legislative action. The gravest danger is that men will belittle our common concerns as "micro" economic issues, as foolish anecdotal information that is meaningless in the face of "macro" economic theories. Key to successful political action, then, will be our ability to make today's leaders see that macro economic decisions do not operate solely in the arena of business and government. They come home almost immediately as issues that trouble women on a daily basis. Women must develop the arguments to close this analytical gap.

African Americans, whose universal opportunity to participate in democracy came only thirty years ago, have always had a visceral understanding of the power of concerted action and have been able to achieve power and influence beyond their numbers. Women have the numbers but need to learn to vote together on the issues that connect them. Women in America have always seen democratic government as a way to achieve a better quality of life for everyone. We have long defined major issues and served on the battle lines—for an end to slavery, for universal suffrage, for civil rights, for protecting the environment, for an end to nuclear arms proliferation. We also show our faith in democracy by consistently voting in ever increasing numbers.

And women do not focus on narrow self-interest—on the candidate who promises to save "me" $200 on taxes this year, for example. Rather we focus on the issues that define us now and in the future: How can I earn enough for my work to provide for my children? How can I find the time to educate my children in the path to responsible adulthood? How can I and everyone I know care for our aging parents and ourselves as we age?

Almost 2,500 years ago, in the play *Lysistrata*, the Greek dramatist Aristophanes imagined women successfully organizing a "sex strike" to force men to make peace with one another. The basic lesson still speaks to all of us: if women work together, there is little we cannot accomplish.

I feel fortunate that I was born here and now, at a time in America when women have seized so much opportunity. I have been able to hand my four children the jewel of that increased opportunity. That jewel is still in the rough, but it can never again be covered or diminished. Its brilliant potential is evident to all. My children's job is to continue the cutting and polishing. Their tools are sharpened and poised, and their buffing cloths are held in skillful and strong hands.

ROSALYNN CARTER has focused her public service career on issues affecting women, children, and people suffering from mental illnesses. As active honorary chair of the President's Commission on Mental Health during the Carter administration, she helped bring about passage of the Mental Health Systems Act of 1980. She chairs the Carter Center Mental Health Task Force and, in 1985, initiated the annual Rosalynn Carter Symposium on Mental Health Policy. In 1991, she cofounded, with Betty Bumpers of Arkansas, "Every Child by Two," a nationwide campaign to publicize the need for early childhood immunization. Her many honors include the Notre Dame Award for International Humanitarian Service, Kiwanis World Service Medal, National Mental Health Association Volunteer of the Decade Award, and the Mental Illness Foundation's Dorothea Dix Award.

Challenges and Change in One Woman's Life

ROSALYNN CARTER

A FEW YEARS AGO, I went to Wesleyan College in Macon, Georgia, to celebrate the 150th anniversary of the first college in the world chartered to grant degrees to women.

In preparation for my remarks that evening, I looked over some of their publications from those early days. One of them was titled "And So It Began." Some of the statements of men opposing "equal educational opportunities for our feminine counterparts" that it quotes are unbelievable to us today, yet this thinking was what women have had to deal with in the past.

When asked for a contribution to the college, one gentleman refused, saying flatly, "I would not have one of your graduates for a wife for I could never even build a pig-pen without her criticizing it and saying it was not put up on mathematical principles."

Another gentleman stated, "No, I will not give a dollar; all a woman needs to know is how to read the New Testament and to spin and weave clothing."

These are two isolated statements, but they point up the difficulty in doing something new and innovative. And it shows what we as women have had to overcome in order to reach the level of equality that we have—or do not have—today.

The change in the role of women in our country has been dramatic and has brought challenges for women that we have not experienced before. And it has happened in a relatively short period of time.

When I was in school, I thought my ultimate prospects for the future were either to get married, if I were lucky, or to be a nurse, a secretary, a school teacher, or maybe a librarian. That doesn't mean that there were no women leaders then or that women didn't achieve. But those whose professional careers exceeded this, or those who became leaders in these professions or in their communities, had just taken their personal situation and made the most of it. They rarely started out to do what they eventually achieved.

Women of that era became experts almost always because of an opportunity or an event in their lives that caused them to become concerned. Perhaps a woman with a mentally retarded child or a sick parent set to work to do something about the needs of her loved one and eventually became the head of a large volunteer agency or of a department of government in the area of her expertise. Or perhaps a woman became concerned about the quality of education available for her children; she began to work, maybe in the PTA, and ended up running for political office, becoming a real influence. These were women who took advantage of their circumstances and became leaders.

Many women do things in their lives that are never publicly acknowledged. That doesn't make the achievement any less. My mother is a good example. When I was thirteen, my father died. I was the oldest of four children; my little sister was only four years old. We were still grieving over the loss of my father when, less than one year later, my mother's mother died.

My mother had always been special and secure and dependent. An only child of doting parents, she married my father who was nine years older and always provided and cared for her. Suddenly she found herself alone with four small children to raise. She did what she had to do; she went to work. She raised us, sending us all to college, which had been my father's wish—on his deathbed, he told her to sell the farm if necessary to send us to school. She took care of her widowed father until he died at age ninety-five. A successful mother, daughter, and expert postal clerk in our local post office, she was an achiever. I am sure that when she was young, she never thought she would someday head a one-parent household and be a working mother.

I don't think I noticed too much how my mother must have been feeling then, but what she taught me by her example has been very important to me all my life. I watched her take charge and do what she had to do. I hadn't realized how much these early experiences affected my later actions and reactions until I wrote my autobiography and was forced to analyze my life in a way that I never had the time or the inclination to do before.

When Jimmy Carter and I married, he was in the Navy. I was very young, and we lived a long way from Plains, Georgia, our tiny rural hometown. During the first two years of our marriage, Jimmy was gone every week from Monday until Friday, and I had to take care of everything. At the end of the first year, I had a baby. I felt overwhelmed, but Jimmy never seemed to worry about me. He assumed that I could manage well and always made me feel that he was proud of me. I was forced to discover that I could do things I never thought I could do, developing in the process a real feeling of independence.

These experiences helped prepare me to accept whatever position I found myself in and to do the best I could with it, whether as the bride of a naval officer or, after coming back home, as the wife of a peanut farmer, learning to be a real business partner, or as first lady of Georgia in the 1970s, understanding for the first time what living in a fishbowl is really like.

Once Jimmy became governor of Georgia, it was ten years before I came home again. Ten years of a life I could never have imagined. There were new experiences every day and new things to learn. Learning, as Georgia's first lady, to make speeches, which I did out of sheer determination; learning not to be so concerned about criticisms (which was good preparation for the White House!) nor to be so intimidated by celebrities; learning that I could make a difference by pursuing the issues I thought were important and tapping the people who could help me most; daring to help Jimmy run for president; then learning through campaigning all over the country what it really means to be an American, and finally, serving our country as first lady. In all of these experiences, I found that there are different ways to learn and meet challenges.

One of my favorite White House stories describes what happened when President Calvin Coolidge invited some friends from his hometown to have dinner with him. It was their first visit to the White House, and they were very nervous about doing everything just right. They got together before the event and decided that they would watch the president and do what he did. The evening arrived, dinner was in progress, and President Coolidge picked up his cup of coffee and poured some into the saucer. His guests all poured coffee into their saucers. He then poured some cream into the saucer. They poured cream into their saucers. Then he put his saucer down on the floor for the cat!

I identify with this story because I have watched, and I have been watched!

In the governor's mansion and in the White House, I have had a chance to work on issues important to women, to work with the mentally afflicted, the elderly, the physically handicapped, the children in inner cities. I learned early that a first lady has influence, and with so many needs in our country, I tried not to waste the opportunities I had.

I have been fortunate all my life. I have always been encouraged, even pushed, to do more sometimes than I thought I could—by my father, by my mother's example, and by Jimmy, who accepted me as a real partner, whether as a wife, a mother, or a co-worker in our business or in special projects at the governor's mansion or the White House.

In thinking about my mother's life and the challenge and change in my life, I have been struck with how much the role of women has changed just in my lifetime. Just look at my daughter, Amy, and the opportunities she has. She is in graduate school, contemplating her future. She can do almost anything she wants to do, become a leader in almost any field—even though it is still mostly a man's world. And these opportunities for her are wonderful.

But her generation also is faced with the challenge of figuring out how to take advantage of these opportunities and still make those contributions to family and community that have always fallen to women: being good mothers, good wives, good neighbors, good leaders in the social activities of the community, such as the PTA and other voluntary organizations. Young women of today have a lot of pressure on them that women never had before.

As a result men are having to recognize the value of what traditionally has been the woman's role and share in the responsibilities of that role. The pressure is on them, too. And society as a whole is going to have to change some attitudes about the so-called responsibilities of women.

We are living at a wonderful time, and our future is bright, but it still depends on how well we meet the challenges that face us. In our fast-changing world, it will take the talents and contributions and leadership of every one of us, women and men alike, to achieve the kind of life all of us want for ourselves and for the generations that come after us.

We have come a long way. We have a long way yet to go.

OUR COLLECTIVE
CHALLENGES

BETTY FORD, first lady of the United States from 1974 to 1977, is president of the board of directors of the Betty Ford Center. A dancer with the Martha Graham Concert Group in New York (1939–1941), she later formed her own dance group in Grand Rapids and taught dance to handicapped children, and her early passion for the dance continues today. As first lady, she focused on the arts, women's issues, and handicapped children, and worked tirelessly for ratification of the ERA. She is the author of *The Times of My Life* (1978) and *Betty: A Glad Awakening* (1987). A trustee of the Martha Graham Dance Center, the Eisenhower Medical Center, and the Nursing Home Advisory Committee, she has received many awards for distinguished service, including the Presidential Medal of Freedom (1991) and honorary doctorates from the University of Michigan and Wesleyan College.

Equal Opportunity for Recovery

BETTY FORD

I AM VERY PROUD that in my lifetime women have gained power and stature in almost every phase of life. We have fought for these changes. They did not come quickly or easily. They were not given to us. We have earned them!

I like the word *empowerment!* You are empowered when you have the capability to control your personal agenda without being penalized. Part of our empowerment is the right to say no. To say no to the candidates who ignore the issues important to us . . . to say no to harassment and unwanted sex . . . to say no to drugs or alcohol. Part of our empowerment is the right to have no understood as an honest answer and not open to interpretation. Yet another part of our empowerment is saying yes when we are in agreement! Our empowerment is feeling comfortable with our choices and secure with each decision.

The changes in our lives as women have also given us the power to be good to ourselves. One of the ways we are being good to ourselves is with our activism over our health care. For example, women are speaking out about medical research, especially about studies based entirely on male subjects. Until recently, medical researchers assumed that the science of women's health would just fall within the findings for men. This assumption has cost millions of women their lives because diagnosis and treatment came too late. As women, we have gained power over our health care. We are no longer ministered to. We are activists, we are outspoken, and we are getting results. Today heart disease is a woman's issue; stroke is a woman's issue; cancer is a woman's issue; AIDS is a woman's issue. And finally, we are being included in the research and the treatment for all the diseases that afflict the human race because we have demanded to be included.

WOMEN'S HEALTH ISSUES IN MY LIFE

I was very fortunate to be involved in two women's health issues, not because I had been on the cutting edge of women's consciousness raising in health care, but through my own personal experience. My position as the wife of the thirty-eighth president of the United States then propelled me to that cutting edge. My experiences with breast cancer and alcoholism brought a new dimension to my life. Recovery helped me develop the survival tools I never knew I had. This discovery provided a new richness, a new feeling of pride in my own being. Part of that richness was the realization that as a woman in an ideal position to speak up, I could help bring about change.

Many Americans still remember the Ford family suddenly moving into 1600 Pennsylvania Avenue in August 1974. The circumstances that led to that move were unusual. Upon the resignation of Vice President Spiro Agnew, my husband, Jerry, had been selected by President Nixon to serve as vice president. Following the turmoil of the Watergate break-in, President Nixon resigned, and Jerry became president of the United States.

My husband's many years as a member of Congress, including ten years as the minority leader in the House, and his service as vice president meant we certainly were not unprepared for our new jobs. It was just not where we had planned to be at that point in our lives. Yes, it was a demanding time for all of us, but we were finding our way. Twenty-five years in Washington gave us fairly comfortable footing for the stresses of being the first family. It was hectic, but we were coping. A month later, all that was dealt a terrible blow. I was diagnosed with breast cancer.

My breast cancer was detected early. My mastectomy and the following chemotherapy were successful in saving my life. By being honest and outspoken in my position as first lady, I was able to change the public perception of breast cancer, to negate some old-fashioned attitudes about mastectomies, and to increase women's awareness of their need for screening for early breast cancer detection.

Breast cancer was something that could be survived. And that survival taught me the value of living each day to the fullest. I learned not to project into the future but to embrace the wonders of today. I gained that very special appreciation that comes when you are not sure how many more days you will be given. These were important qualities to have when I found myself confronted with another health issue a few years later.

In 1978, alcoholism—specifically a dependence on prescription drugs and alcohol—became a woman's health care issue for me. On April l, 1978, my family confronted me in what is known as an intervention. It was an action precipitated by the bonds of love. Love that was so strong it made my family want to do something to help me. Love that enabled them to look beyond their own intense fear and denial and push through to confront me with my own denial of my disease. My family finally came to the realization that they had to do something if I was to survive. I will be forever grateful that they had the courage and the love to face me that morning.

Yes, I was ill, and I was seeing a physician for the discomfort I suffered from back and neck pain. But the painkillers, the muscle relaxants, and the tranquilizers, augmented by a couple of evening cocktails, made it impossible for me to see or feel how far I had slipped into the disease of alcoholism.

When the members of my family walked in on that beautiful April morning, my first thought was, "What a wonderful surprise. Everyone's come home to see me." My second thought was, "Good heavens, something really important must be going on." You see, unbeknownst to me, they had come from across the country to tell me that as a family, we shared more than just our love. We also shared a very serious problem, a problem we had to face, a problem we had to address. And of course, that problem was my alcoholism.

They told me that my disease was not only a burden to me but to them as well. It was destroying our lives together as a family. At the time, I was surprised and shocked, even angry, at what they were saying. It was painful to hear what they were telling me. They spoke of specific occasions when my actions had bewildered and distressed them. They outlined missed dinners, forgotten conversations, and damaged feelings. With a great deal of caring and concern, they let me know they were no longer willing to make excuses and be a part of the denial of my alcoholism. Nor were they willing to watch my disease progress.

I had always taken great pride in the devotion and dedication I had given my family. I truly believed that my life had been lived for each of them. Now all I could hear was that I had let them down, that I had failed them as a wife and mother. I was devastated.

Even so, through all the tears and anger, there was something else I heard them saying. Yes, even in my despair, I could hear them telling me that they loved me too much to let me go. That was what caught my attention. The outcome? Well, together we decided that I would attend the alcohol and drug treatment program at Long Beach Naval Hospital.

WOMEN AND CHEMICAL DEPENDENCY

When I entered the hospital, I discovered I was unique. Unique because I was a former first lady, of course, but just as noticeably because I was a woman. There were very few women openly talking about alcoholism as "their" disease. The few alcohol treatment facilities available were directing their programs to men patients. It just was not socially acceptable for a woman to be an alcoholic or to seek recovery. The national mind-set did not include a picture of a woman dependent on alcohol and drugs. So most women remained hidden in their denial, a denial intensified by the conspiracy of silence within their families. The woman alcoholic could not be acknowledged or discussed. Her alcoholism was ignored; maybe it would go away, and nobody would notice. Certainly it was an embarrassment to the family.

Because there were so few women in treatment, they remained an underserved minority. A woman in search of treatment and recovery was simply an oddity who had to fit into the programs already in existence. For all of history, I suppose, there has been a general belief that alcoholism was a man's disease. Since only men sought treatment, since only men were in support groups, perhaps, it was thought, they were more susceptible to alcoholism's destructive nature.

We have long lived with a stereotype of what a woman should be, what her role in her family and her community should be. A woman was a dutiful daughter, a loving wife, a devoted mother. She was put on the pedestal reserved for the female of the species, and that pedestal required perfection. She was expected to go through the day untouched and unaffected by the troubles and turmoil of life because it was believed she was to be taken care of and protected by a man.

As an alcoholic, a woman did not meet the image created by the stereotype. Somehow she had failed at achieving female perfection. And no one wants to admit to failure.

Until very recently, we women grew up receiving negative and confused messages about our roles and our capabilities. Far too many of us have lived our lives in fulfilling the demands of what we should be rather than the reality of what we are. Being chemically dependent was certainly not included in those demands. So if we were alcoholic, we were quick to believe there was something very wrong, very shameful, and very crazy about our lives. We brought these negative beliefs with us to treatment. Now, as more and more women seek treatment, as more and more women are encouraged to find out what they could be, this distorted vision of the "good woman" and the "bad woman" is changing.

Fortunately for me, while I was in treatment I was helped by a special group of recovering women. They came to the hospital once a week and shared their feelings, their experiences, and their joy of recovery with me. Through this group of attractive, successful, and caring women, I began to accept myself not as an oddity but as a woman with a dependency on prescription drugs and alcohol, a woman alcoholic. I learned I was allergic to all mood-altering substances. These women were strong and happy and proud in their recovery. They knew very well how this disease can stigmatize and degrade a woman. They understood that with this stigma and the powerful denial that is part of the disease, getting women into treatment and continued recovery was a very complex problem.

Until very recently, no one wanted to accept that there were more and more of us affected by alcoholism, but we were. We were not asking for help, however, because of the social and cultural implications of the disease.

But there is more than acceptance and self-worth to be addressed for the woman alcoholic. Research is now finding specific proof that men and women with alcoholism have very different physical reactions. For one thing, any drugs we women take are more rapidly assimilated by our organs and become quickly concentrated in our bodies. Scientists also have identified a stomach enzyme that plays an important part in metabolizing and breaking down alcohol. And guess what? Women have less of this enzyme; so 30 percent more of the alcohol we consume gets to our bloodstream.

When I was in treatment, I learned that alcoholism is a progressive disease, and for women, the progression is more rapid. The net effect is called telescoping. We usually begin our drinking later in life than men do, yet we end up in need of help at approximately the same age and with many more physical problems. But even with its greater physical repercussions, our disease and its progression may continue to be overlooked—just because we are women.

The woman who is pregnant and uses drugs and alcohol plays a doubly dangerous game. The drugs she takes pass directly through the umbilical cord to the fetus, which can suffer intensified damage from the resulting chemical imbalance. Prenatal exposure to alcohol can cause death through spontaneous abortion and stillbirth. Fetal alcohol syndrome and fetal alcohol effects can often result in facial distortions, damaged hearts, stunted growth, retardation, and hyperactivity. In the last few years, infant cerebral palsy has been linked to drug and alcohol use in pregnancy.

The most obvious difference between men and women is the monthly hormonal change a woman experiences. As we learn more and more about premenstrual syndrome (PMS), we are becoming aware of its implications for a woman using drugs and alcohol. The monthly changes in a woman's estrogen level can heighten and prolong the effect of the drugs she takes. Her mood swings also may be greatly intensified when chemicals are ingested. Today's treatment for drug dependency is designed to take these purely female characteristics into consideration.

Many estimates indicate that of the 15 million Americans who are alcoholic, six million are women. This is more than one-third of all those who are chemically dependent. My own experience at the Betty Ford Center suggests an even higher ratio. Since the center opened its doors, 40 to 50 percent of its patients have been women. The higher percentage of women at the center may be because it bears a woman's name—or it may be because the center shows a truer reflection of the alcoholic population. What shocks me most is that as part of our changing life-styles, the percentage of young women (aged twenty-one to thirty-four) who drink heavily has doubled in the past twenty years. Women now start their drinking as teenagers, just as they begin smoking at a younger age than the previous generation did. These young women must be encouraged to find help. We cannot afford to ignore them. They must be offered the support that was so generously given to me all those years ago.

At the Betty Ford Center, treatment is individualized for all patients, both male and female. After all, alcoholism is an equal opportunity disease. The opportunity for recovery should be equal as well. Besides, as a liberated woman, I thought it only fair to give the men an even break. The center does provide small groups for "women only"; women in co-ed therapy groups seem inclined to fall into their traditional role of caretaker. In mixed groups, they are more likely to focus on men and on the problems of men, leaving their own needs unattended. In women's groups, a woman feels relieved of her traditional role and better able to begin to share more openly, to look more honestly at her failures and successes.

Within her own peer group, a woman deals more easily with her anger, guilt, shame, and resentment. She can examine her feelings of depression and begin to build and regain her self-esteem. She feels more comfortable talking about gender-sensitive issues such as incest, rape, and sexual abuse. This sharing with other women allows her more easily to accept her disease and work toward recovery. Once a woman leaves treatment, she is expected to establish herself with a support group within her own community, a twelve-step program such as Alcoholics Anonymous.

An old adage in recovery is "If you don't want to slip, you should stay away from slippery places." This means staying away from the places and the people that were part of your drinking and drug-using life-style. For a woman, this can be almost impossible. Because that slippery place was probably her own home—her kitchen, her bedroom, or her office. The people who were around when she was drinking or using were most often the members of her family or her co-workers. When I left Long Beach, I knew I needed and wanted the support of other recovering women. Such support of others is an ongoing principle for anyone in recovery. I was told in treatment that my disease is "alcoholism," not "alcoholwasm." This disease is progressive, it is chronic, and it can be fatal. There is no cure, but it is one of the most treatable of all illnesses.

Awareness makes us all stronger. The more you know and understand, the more aware you are of the stigma every woman suffers when dealing with alcoholism, the better you will be able to encourage another woman when she reaches out for help.

As women, many of us have the added delights and pressures of being mothers and grandmothers. There are many ways in which we have the opportunity and the obligation to be positive, inspiring role models for the children in our lives. I think most of us realize that our youngsters look to us with bright, eager, unsophisticated eyes. They are anxious to copy the lead we offer. "Do as I say, not as I do" can be an almost impossible rule to place on a child. The adult who tells a child not to drink and then drinks and drives herself or himself is sending a very confused message. The parent who says, "Thank goodness, my kid doesn't do drugs; he only drinks beer," may feel that this level of alcoholic behavior is okay for a teenager. But for those under twenty-one, beer is an illegal substance.

Beer and marijuana are considered gateway drugs for other more powerful drugs. The use of gateway drugs cannot be accepted or condoned as only a part of growing up. Our children must learn that it isn't glamorous or fun to use drugs; it is dangerous and deadly. It is important both that we be role models for our children and that we show the young people in our lives how valued they are. The future is theirs, and they need to grow with a concept of their own worth, to know, absolutely, that they are extremely valuable to their families, to their friends, and to themselves. You and I have a responsibility to answer the questions our children raise. Some of those questions can be pretty tough. If you're not prepared, dealing with questions about drugs and alcohol can make that timeless question "Where do babies come from?" seem like a piece of cake!

I have a very wise friend, a man who is recovering and who played a very important role in the establishment of the Betty Ford Center. He has always said to me, "You know, Betty, it isn't a sin to be an alcoholic. The sin is in being one and not doing something about it." To that I can only add, Amen!

BERNADINE HEALY is dean of the Ohio State University College of Medicine. As director of the National Institutes of Health (1991–1993), she launched the Women's Health Initiative to study diseases affecting women. She was chair of the Cleveland Clinic Foundation Research Institute (1985–1991), deputy director of the White House Office of Science and Technology Policy (1984–1985), and professor at Johns Hopkins University School of Medicine (1976–1984), where she had completed her postgraduate training in internal medicine and cardiology after graduating from Vassar College and Harvard Medical School. She is the author of *A New Prescription for Women's Health: Getting the Best Medical Care in a Man's World* (1995). She was also president of the American Federation of Clinical Research (1983–1984) and the American Heart Association (1988–1989).

Harvard Medicine in the Women's Era

BERNADINE HEALY

IN THE SUMMER OF 1944, the very summer I was born, the
Harvard overseers were waging a battle as they deliberated a momentous decision to overcome an age-old prejudice against women
in medicine. The culmination of their battle appeared in the September 26, 1944, *New York Times:* "Harvard opened the doors of its Medical School to women today for the first time since the school was
founded 162 years ago. Closing a long fight, the Board of Overseers of
Harvard College approved a recommendation . . . that women be eligible for admission." The newspaper went on to explain that the over-

Note: This chapter is based in part on remarks delivered at the Harvard Medical
School 1995 graduation ceremony and also on my book *A New Prescription for
Women's Health: Getting the Best Medical Care in a Man's World.*

seers justified their action on the grounds of patriotism. And so began
what I like to call the Women's Era at Harvard Medical School.

Living in Queens, my family had the *New York Times* as their home
newspaper. Little did my parents know that the action described in that
page twenty report would affect their newborn daughter, making it
possible for little Bernie's application to Harvard Medical School to be
accepted some twenty years later (without pretending, like Yentl, that
Bernie was a boy). I am convinced, however, that my parents never read
that momentous column. It was on the woman's page, almost obscured
by the surrounding articles on town and country wear, cosmetics made
easier, news of unusual foods, and a picture of the 1944 version of the
Wonder Bra (some things haven't changed). Now it is not just that fash-
ion, beauty, and gourmet food overwhelmed the successful fight to get
women admitted to Harvard Medical School; it's just that all these
events were surely dwarfed by the real news of the day, World War II.

The rest of that day's paper was dominated by war stories. On the
front page alone were reports of the Americans and British pouring
monster shells over the Siegfried line at the Nazis; the Red Army had
nearly completed the liberation of Estonia; a Navy plane called *Black
Cat* sank three Japanese war ships in the South Pacific; and Charles de
Gaulle announced that the war was likely to go on until the spring. Also
on the very same page was a story about the mudslinging battles between President Roosevelt and Governor Dewey—yes, 1944 was also
a presidential election year.

Actually the war and its many battles are not so far removed from
the decision that allowed me to attend Harvard Medical School. G.I.
Joe may have won the war in Europe and the Pacific; Roosevelt may
have won his battle for reelection; but the silent hero of the day was
Rosie the Riveter, who started a revolution. Rosie was the poster image
for patriotic women moving into such traditionally male jobs as "man-
ning" heavy equipment, building airplanes and cars, and driving
trucks—all as part of the war effort.

Rosie's kind of fervor was also needed to help terminate a more difficult home-front battle: women doctors' struggles to get military com-

missions. Since the War Department interpreted the "persons" that they could legally commission into the Army to mean men only, it took both a desperate need and an act of Congress to enable the commissioning of women into the Army and Navy Medical Corps. That change occurred in 1943, a full two years before Harvard Medical School opened its doors to women.

So in truth, it was Rosie's revolution that really led the overseers of Harvard to end their fight to keep women out of Harvard medicine. Their decision was based on war need rather than faith in the abilities of women to prevail academically, in battle, or in physical performance. (But, hey, we'll still take it.)

Women had to have stamina: their battle for admission to Harvard spanned a full century. The idea first surfaced in 1847 when Dr. Oliver Wendell Holmes, the first dean of the medical school and father of the renowned jurist, proposed that women be permitted to attend medical school lectures; his proposal was resoundingly rejected. In 1872, Harvard had a second chance but dismissed a proposal to have a Female Medical College. Yet another proposal was turned down during World War I. In 1949, the first year women graduated from Harvard Medical School, the *New York Times* editorialized about women attending Harvard's professional schools (law now, as well as medicine): "The time when women's brains were considered on the average inferior to men's is long past. What is left is only superstition."

THE POSTWAR ERA

The men and women at Harvard Medical School have a lot to be proud of since the time the overseers made their momentous decision. Medicine of the past fifty years is about medical research transforming the medical world, about practice translating that research into all kinds of human benefit.

World War II altered the field of medicine in immeasurable ways: not just in its view of women in medicine but in its very focus and practice. Just like the face of the medical school student body, the very face of today's medicine was fashioned by the World War II era and the events of the immediate postwar years.

During World War II, President Franklin Roosevelt declared that after the war our nation should direct the power of science and technology, which was so critical to winning the war, toward civilian goals. Science was dubbed "the endless frontier." Roosevelt—perhaps because he knew firsthand the suffering of chronic debilitating disease—singled out medicine above all the sciences as the national pursuit that would bring maximal benefit to the lives of all Americans. To achieve the common good, the next war was to be the war on human disease; the ramparts America watched became medical, not just military.

During that active, hopeful time, the National Institutes of Health (NIH) were developed, intentionally separate from the other areas of science. Because of its crucial mission to protect and improve the health of the public, medical research was not funded as part of the National Science Foundation (NSF), as some advised at the time, but apart. One measure of the importance of that half-century-old political decision is that NSF is now a $3 billion agency while the NIH budget exceeds $11 billion annually. You don't have to be in medicine to see just how that investment has paid off. It's simple. Just look at those postwar years of the 1950s and compare them to today.

We all hear about the wonderful fifties. My teenage daughter has fifties parties. This was a glorious time in our history: our economy was expanding, our country was prosperous, we had peace at home, and through the Marshall Plan, we were helping Europe rebuild.

But for our physical and mental health, those times were not so glorious. We were in the midst of an epidemic of heart attacks and sudden deaths among middle-aged men, an epidemic that we didn't understand. Cancer was an unspeakable, incurable disease. Those with severe mental illness were seen as hopelessly insane. Growing up in Queens in the 1950s, I used to look down on a mysterious edifice on a little island I could see at a distance as I crossed the Queensborough Bridge—it was called the Hospital for the Incurably Ill. I imagined it to be a scary place, an Alcatraz for the sick and disabled.

The sick were too often discarded back then. Not because we did not value them but because we did not have the means to help them. There was no heart surgery to make blue babies pink, prevent heart attacks, or replace deformed heart valves. We did not have cardiac pacemakers, artificial hips or knees, kidney dialysis, or organ transplantation. We had no effective treatments for high blood pressure, no chemotherapy or radiation treatment for cancer. Penicillin was a miracle breakthrough of the war years, but it remained essentially the only antibiotic we had. Rheumatic fever was still rampant among our children. Frontal lobotomy was being celebrated worldwide as a breakthrough treatment for severe depression, a treatment that won a Nobel Prize.

And then there was polio. President Roosevelt used a wheelchair because of it. I vividly remember summer fears of polio. More than once, the health officials closed the public swimming pool in our neighborhood because of the risk of polio. I recall the fear in all the mothers each time one of their children had a summer fever or sore throat. And there was Louie, who lived next door to us and got polio. He survived but was left paralyzed. How far we have come these many years from the glorious fifties.

Those in medicine have a lot to be proud of when they think back to those times not so very long ago. Medical research and innovation have revolutionized people's lives. We now can cure many cancers and treat virtually all of them. Polio is no longer the summer dirge of the nation's cities. We have seen dramatic decreases in mortality from heart disease and stroke. Neuropharmaceuticals targeted at selective brain chemicals for treatment of depression and anxiety have superseded lobotomy. And these past successes have only increased our expectations for doing better and doing it faster for the many challenges we still face.

But those successes did not occur by accident. It was by choice that medicine and medical research in this country became a priority. As a nation, we spend a trillion dollars a year on our health. We invest over $11 billion in biomedical research through the National Institutes of Health and another $13 billion to $14 billion through private-sector research by industry to sustain the present advances in medicine and to cure the illnesses of tomorrow. This sustained, unwavering investment in medical care and innovation is part of that strategic commitment to health made almost fifty years ago.

And that is why the United States leads the world in advanced health care but also why that care is so expensive. As one wag aptly noted: "In the rest of the world, death is inevitable; in the U.S., it's an option." We have been striving to produce the best at whatever cost. Modern medicine has changed our *expectations* of life as much as our quality of life and length of life.

TOMORROW'S PRACTICE

As we look to the next fifty years, we will see even more profound transformations of our world by virtue of discoveries in biology and medicine. The powers of molecular and structural biology and biotechnology suggest an endless frontier. No human disease should be safe from extinction or radical control. Genetically engineered cancer vaccines hold the promise of destroying even the most advanced and spreading tumors. Reconstituting the human immune system will allow AIDS victims to live with their disease.

Learning how to destroy human viruses lurking within living human cells will bring us cures for HIV, hepatitis, many tumors, and even, at long last, the common cold. Understanding, delaying, preventing, or curing Alzheimer's disease would not only help four million Americans today but also, given the predicted growth of that disease, could save the sixteen million Americans projected to have this disease by the year 2040.

We are mapping the human genome, the command and control center that carries the biological code for much of who we are. Molecular medicine will rewrite the textbooks of tomorrow. We have already discovered genes for cystic fibrosis and colon and breast cancer; we have linked genes to prostate cancer, osteoporosis, and some forms of heart disease. In time, we will understand the genetic determinants of addictive behavior, common forms of atherosclerosis, manic-depressive illness, and maybe even intelligence and artistic talent.

With each discovery comes the understanding to detect, delay, and cure disease and the understanding of more and more about the nature of life, human and otherwise. Our world will surely change in the process. Much of what we know about human biology and many of the health decisions made in the field of medicine today will be markedly different in the future. Some of the changes seem obvious and are the price of success. For example, the patients doctors treat will be *older.* More Americans will be pushing up against a probable human life span of one hundred years. That is positive news for people who can remain fit and engaged in productive activity in their later years but a depressing thought if longer lives mean more time in nursing homes, the bankrupting of Social Security and Medicare, and a wave of tenured professors with Alzheimer's.

Physicians will treat *more chronic disease.* As a corollary to living longer, chronic disease will increase. Women already face more chronic diseases than men, due in part to the fact they live seven or eight years longer. Osteoporosis, arthritis, stroke, heart failure, dementias, and recurrent cancers will demand our attention as never before. The focus in research and practice will be as much on quality of life as on quantity of life.

More preventive medicine will be practiced, but it will be *high-technology prevention.* Let me be contrarian to the voices out there that claim prevention is the cheapest form of medicine. That's true if we are talking about yesterday's prevention: practicing good hygiene and sanitation, exercising, eating a low-fat diet, not smoking, and watching one's weight and blood pressure. But that is only a small part of the prevention we will practice in the future. Look at some recent trends: a lifetime of cholesterol-lowering agents for some patients with intractably high serum cholesterol levels; hormone replacement for women and maybe for men, not for two years but for twenty or thirty; prophylactic colectomy for those under forty with familial polyposis. As we more precisely define risk in genetic terms, we will feel the obligation to do something, long before any disease appears. In the words of one breast cancer survivor following the recent much-awaited, lauded, and celebrated discovery of a breast cancer gene: "So what, if all it does is tell a woman she will get breast cancer when there is nothing she can do about it!"

The point is that we will be compelled in most cases to find out what to do about it. And that means treating diseases before they occur. If a gene within an individual is viewed as a ticking time bomb, that perception may translate into mastectomy or ovary removal or years of drug treatment before any disease appears. Will discovery of the prostate cancer gene lead to prophylactic prostate removal or its pharmacological equivalent in men of an early middle age?

Extending high-tech diagnosis and prophylactic treatment to diseases we do not yet have will have its pluses but also its minuses. The economic cost of health care will surely rise and, in all likelihood, so will the prevalence of both anxiety and depression, prompting excursions into yet more preventive interventions—perhaps prophylactic Prozac.

As we imagine all the many advances we will encounter in the medicine of tomorrow, we also must pause in awe of the power of tomorrow's medical and life sciences to transform the world in which we live and the ways in which we think. For medical science to continue to flourish and realize all the dreams of tomorrow, we must acknowledge now that ethics and the public interest will more and more become the companions of science wherever science goes.

People who read *Jurassic Park*—written by my Harvard Medical School classmate Michael Crichton—were entertained by the fiction of genetics and biotechnology gone mad. But there was a sobering thought voiced by one of the main characters: "We are witnessing the end of the scientific era." It is our responsibility and that of the next generation to assure that this fictional apocalypse does not occur. Today's medical school graduates will come face to face with a whole new realm of dilemmas driven by science that earlier generations fretted about only in science fiction or in ivory towers. Here are a few examples:

People are being asked to make harder and harder beginning- and end-of-life decisions. Living wills that specify whether one is to be kept alive by artificial means are becoming common practice; such wills defined medical choices in the final weeks of life for both Richard Nixon and Jacqueline Kennedy Onassis. However, we also see, stepping far over the line of professional ethics, Dr. Jack Kevorkian. He and his supporters chillingly seek to redefine the role of physician to include destroyer of depressed and suffering souls who ask to die.

Genetic therapy on somatic cells is here. How will we define the limits of gene therapy on gametes, which constitute the gene pool that will carry any perturbations it experiences faithfully into future generations, whether we like it or not?

Growing human embryos in the laboratory for research purposes is already the subject of hot debate. Now under a moratorium, this research is currently banned from NIH support. Nonetheless, two distinguished academic panels have tried hard to get government support for such experimentation, and it is only a matter of time before the issue surfaces again.

Young college women are actively being procured for egg donation through ads in college newspapers. In some cases, the ads solicit a specific religious background and physical type in the egg bearer. Some young women are being lured by the offer of thousands of dollars, but the full long-term impact of the donation procedure on the paid donor's health is by no means clear.

Genetic privacy is becoming a matter of concern. What if we can define a gene for alcoholism, schizophrenia, or some other behavioral feature that might be phenotypically—that is, visibly—expressed in some individuals but never affect the others who carry it? What are the implications for life insurance, health insurance, job applications? Certain genetic codes could become new sources of prejudice.

Designer children are not an impossibility. Although the possibility that we could check out the characteristics of an unborn child by a sort of virtual reality projection is further off than any of the other scenarios listed here, it is no longer science fiction to imagine what might be done once we are able to describe an individual's entire genetic makeup.

In a March 1995 article in the journal *Science,* which "blue-skied" about future scientific developments, Dr. Harvey Lodish, a distinguished molecular biologist from the Whitehead Institute and MIT, made this provocative prediction:

> By using techniques involving in vitro fertilization, it is already possible to remove one cell from the developing embryo and characterize any desired region of DNA. Genetic screening of embryos, before implantation, may soon become routine. It will be possible, by sequencing important regions of the mother's DNA, to infer important properties of the egg from which the person develops. . . . [T]his information will be transferred to a super-computer, together with information about the environment—including likely nutrition, environmental toxins, sunlight and so forth. The output will be a color movie in which the embryo develops into a fetus, is born, and then grows into an adult, explicitly depicting body size and shape and hair, skin, and eye color. Eventually the DNA sequence base will be expanded to cover genes important for traits such as speech and musical ability; the mother will be able to hear the embryo—as an adult—speak or sing.

A breathtaking notion. That embryo-adult in virtual reality on your supercomputer is your future generation looking back at you through a crystal ball. But what happens if in virtual reality she sings badly or talks back? Or what if you don't want a brown-eyed brunette, or a crook in her nose, or freckles on her face? What will you do, inevitably armed as you will be with high-technology prevention and gene therapy? Crystal balls are supposed to show you the future; up to now, they have not usually given you the chance to change it.

Our astounding successes in science and medicine will bring us joy and benefit but also problems. Think about it. Today we are confronting the economic challenge, the dollar cost, of the extraordinary successes of biological and medical research. But tomorrow we will confront new kinds of ethical, social, and moral challenges that will make the economic problems that seize the headlines now seem simple and the battles over whether or not to admit women into medical school seem downright petty.

What this medical world of tomorrow will demand is a generation of informed leadership in research and practice; people who have the courage and the wisdom to get the ethical, social, and moral issues right. It will take knowing what we stand for in ethical and moral terms. It will take persistence and disciplined thought and broad debate throughout society, way beyond the ivory tower. It will require us as researchers, as clinicians, and as fully engaged members of a changing society to follow new paths. It will take the wisdom and perspective of women as well as of men, working together on matters that no one man or one woman could even begin to face alone.

I wonder if Rosie the Riveter knows just how critical her revolution has been for medicine.

DONNA SHALALA is secretary of the Department of Health and Human Services. From 1988 to 1993, she was chancellor of the University of Wisconsin at Madison, the first woman to head a Big Ten University. She was president of Hunter College for eight years, assistant secretary for policy development and research at the Department of Housing and Urban Development (1977–1980), and director and treasurer of the Municipal Assistance Corporation in New York (1975–1977). She was one of the first Peace Corps volunteers in Iran, from 1962 to 1964. For more than a decade, she was on the board of the Children's Defense Fund, serving as chair in 1992. In 1995, she cochaired the U.S. delegation to the U.N. Fourth World Conference on Women. She is a graduate of Western College for Women and earned a Ph.D. degree from the Maxwell School of Citizenship and Public Affairs at Syracuse University.

Our Collective Challenges

DONNA SHALALA

I N 1979, AT A National Women's Political Caucus convention in
Cincinnati, I listened attentively as Patricia Roberts Harris—then
the secretary of Housing and Urban Development and soon to be secretary of Health and Human Services—delivered a moving call to arms.
Like Secretary Harris, I now sit with the cabinet at the president's State
of the Union address and dream and work for the day in the next century when the speaker of the house is addressed as Madam Speaker—
and she introduces Madam President.

Note: This chapter is excerpted from a speech to the National Women's Political Caucus Convention, August 5, 1995, and testimony before the U.S. Senate Subcommittee on Labor, Health and Human Services, Education and Related Agencies, August
10, 1995.

We have travelled great distances since that day in 1979. We have taken many steps forward and some backward.

Seared in our collective memories is the spectacle—the very absolute spectacle—of an all-male Judiciary Committee of the United States Senate questioning Anita Hill and Clarence Thomas on the issue of sexual harassment. That was 1991; after the 1992 election, two women became members of the Senate Judiciary Committee.

Before the 1992 election, Republican Nancy Kassebaum of Kansas and Democrat Barbara Mikulski of Maryland were the only women in the United States Senate. As Dianne Feinstein explained in her 1992 campaign for election to the Senate from California: "Two percent is fine for milk—but not for the U.S. Senate!" By 1995, the number of women in the Senate reached eight—Republicans and Democrats alike. In 1979, only sixteen women served in the U.S. House of Representatives; in 1995, forty-seven women were in the House. We have now doubled the number of women in state legislatures and more than tripled the number of women mayors.

Seven women hold cabinet-level positions in the Clinton administration, including the first woman attorney general, the first woman national economic adviser, the first woman secretary of the Department of Energy, and the first woman director of the Office of Management and Budget. More women are serving as judges than ever before; 53 percent of President Clinton's appointees—from district court to the Supreme Court—have been women and minorities.

Have we taken giant steps forward? Yes, we have. But even as we celebrate these accomplishments, are we in danger of losing precious ground? You bet we are.

In 1979, Secretary Harris warned that "we will be ridiculed and parodied, because if our cause is right and cannot be destroyed, those who oppose our cause will seek to destroy our credibility." Just ask Anita Hill whether that is still true today.

It was on August 26, 1920, that we women guaranteed our voices would be heard through the bullhorn of the ballot. Since that day, our history has been a steady march of progress as year by year, in many different ways, we have climbed new mountains, and secured new rights. So it is ironic that we must talk about one of the biggest threats to our progress ever launched in history. This is not an isolated attack. It is a systematic assault to turn back the clock and bring back the days of darkness.

Let's begin with the issue of welfare reform. We believe that welfare ought to be about helping people get jobs—and keep them. Unfortunately there are some in Congress and the statehouses who want to use this issue to divide our country, point fingers at the vulnerable, and leave children out in the cold. And that's wrong.

- When they refer to women on welfare as "wolves" devouring our resources—stigmatizing poor women and blaming the victim—we must say no.
- When they punish poor children for their parents' mistakes—we must say no.
- When they take away the tools women need—like child care, training, and education—to get off welfare and stay off, when they destroy the safety net, when they refuse to raise the minimum wage, we must say no.

Our opponents do not stop with welfare. They also want to abandon a commitment to family planning that is more than a quarter century old. Abolishing family planning services reminds me of the old saying that the difference between genius and stupidity is that genius has its limits.

There simply is no limit to the stupidity of taking away health care services that help women *prevent* unplanned pregnancies, *prevent* abortions, and *prevent* diseases. Would these people take us back to the days when Margaret Sanger had to walk through the tenements of New York City dispensing birth control from her purse because no one else would? In 1916, Sanger opened a birth control clinic in an extremely poor slum in Brooklyn. Women lined up outside the clinic to receive services; after nine days, the clinic had seen 464 women. On the tenth day, Sanger and her two assistants were arrested, and all their supplies and files were confiscated.

We cannot take our country back to the days when poor women got back-alley abortions because they could not afford birth control. We cannot—and we will not—return to those days of desperation, disfigurement, and sometimes even death. In 1970, when the Title X Family Planning Program was created with strong bipartisan support, Congressman Robert A. Taft, Jr., Republican of Ohio, promised that the program would help us take "a major step toward meeting . . . the family planning needs of . . . 5.4 million lower income American families." Those needs are more important than ever today.

When we talk about the federal government's only program dedicated to family planning, we need to separate fiction from fact. Title X opponents want Americans to believe that Title X family-planning dollars go to abortion services. Nothing could be farther from the truth. Ever since Title X was enacted, its programs have been prohibited from using Title X money to pay for abortions. What Title X money *is* spent for is a range of family-planning and preventive health services—like contraceptive devices and pap smears, physical exams and blood pressure screenings—provided for over four million women and men in more than four thousand clinics nationwide. The money also provides educational materials to hundreds of community groups and religious organizations across the country to help young people say no to sex. And it helps train two hundred and fifty certified family-planning nurse practitioners each year.

When we discuss Title X, we should look at the human faces—the four million faces—behind the issue. These citizens are our sons and daughters, our neighbors and our friends. They are

- A newly married couple in Philadelphia—who are finishing their education and aren't ready to start a family.
- A thirty-year-old store clerk in St. Louis—who doesn't have health insurance and can't qualify for Medicaid.

- A forty-year-old mother of two in Greenville—who depends upon a Title X clinic for her annual gynecological checkups.

These people all have something in common: they may be just one unintended pregnancy away from poverty, unemployment, and welfare.

To those who say we cannot afford to spend our resources on family planning, I say we can't afford not to.

For every dollar we spend on family planning we save more than four dollars in medical care, welfare benefits, and other social services. That's what I call a good investment.

What a big mistake it would be to force Title X clinics—sometimes the only family-planning provider in a community—to shut their doors and turn off their lights. What a mistake it would be to dismantle our family-planning system and send the message that we don't care about clinics that provide low-income men and women with preventive health care. And what a mistake it would be to take us down a dangerous road leading to

- More abortions
- More parents and children living in poverty and on welfare
- More unintended pregnancies
- Higher rates of infant mortality
- More people living without the security of critical preventive care like pap smears, mammograms, and screening for sexually transmitted diseases

We don't need to turn back the clocks on the health of our families. We need a much different approach. We need to maintain our bipartisan commitment to the families of America while also giving states the flexibility they need to prioritize their resources and provide local services.

That is exactly what we are accomplishing with the Title X program. We are operating in the pro-family tradition by working to ensure that every pregnancy and every child is wanted. Family planning is about ensuring that every pregnancy is a planned one and that all children are born healthy into loving and supportive families. Family planning is about preventing unintended pregnancies, decreasing abortions, lowering infant mortality rates, and improving the health of families and their children.

That is our collective challenge.

Those who want to take us backward are also proposing to slash Medicare and Medicaid. This is a threat to every American woman and family. Too many of our sisters and mothers do not realize that these cuts add up to something truly radical—a blindside charge on our hard-won rights and our much-needed health security.

- We are the ones who make up almost 60 percent of the Medicare and Medicaid population—more than thirty million women strong.
- We are the ones whose life expectancy is almost seven years longer than men's.
- We are the ones who typically rely on home care to stay out of a nursing home.
- We are the ones who are more likely to end up quitting our jobs and becoming full-time caregivers if—God forbid—one of our loved ones gets tossed out of a nursing home for lack of money.

We are almost at the dawn of a new century. We will not go back.

We will not go back to the days when seniors had to choose between eating and getting decent health care. We will not go back to the days when our grandmothers brought bags of apples to pay the doctor. The future of Medicare and Medicaid is about nothing less than our future as women. It is about every family's security; it is about the future of our country.

This is not a choice between left and right. This is a choice between right and wrong. This is more than a choice between moving forward or falling back. This is a choice between life and death.

So as we celebrate seventy-five years of woman suffrage, we must gird ourselves for one more battle in this century. This is it—the final assault, the final campaign to destroy the modern American women's movement.

The threat we face is not a campaign to destroy feminism. Our enemies are putting on their armor to end opportunity and decent lives and fairness for waitresses in Topeka and corporate executives in New York. This is not a class war: every American family, rich or poor, will lose if our opponents win.

This is a fight for hard-working families, for our children, for our daughters *and* our sons. It is a fight for old and young, strong and weak. It is about race, gender, sexual orientation, and disability. It is about Asian and African, Native American and Hispanic. It is about all of us—Republicans and Democrats.

This is a great country because it is a good country. We are good to our people; we do not play politics with their lives and their futures.

The stakes are high and women's voices must be heard. Every activist woman I know has made enormous personal and professional sacrifices for the cause of equality and opportunity. Many of them are battle weary. So am I. But women made a nation listen before. We have won before, and we will win again.

We will win in the names of women like Alice Paul, Sojourner Truth, Susan B. Anthony, Carrie Chapman Catt, Frances Perkins, Mary McLeod Bethune, and the countless others—women and men, Republicans and Democrats—who opened up the steel doors with their sacrifices and courage in factories and offices and homes. On battlefields and playing fields, they stepped up so that all of us could walk right through to the dream—and the opportunity—of this extraordinary country.

For them and for America, we must step up once more. Because, as Secretary Harris said that day in 1979: "Our goal of full equality is still well ahead of us."

ANTONIA HERNÁNDEZ is president and general counsel of the
Mexican American Legal Defense and Educational Fund
(MALDEF). She began her professional legal career as a staff at-
torney with the Los Angeles Center for Law and Justice in 1974.
From 1977 to 1979, she was directing attorney for the Lincoln
Heights office of the Legal Aid Foundation of Los Angeles. She
was staff counsel to the Senate Committee on the Judiciary from
January 1979 to December 1980. Her board service includes the
National Hispanic Leadership Agenda, National Endowment for
Democracy, Independent Sector, and Manpower Demonstration
Research Corporation. She is a graduate of the University of
California at Los Angeles and the UCLA School of Law, which
has established the Antonia Hernández Public Service Award for
its graduates.

Whose Nation Is This?

ANTONIA HERNÁNDEZ

A T A TIME WHEN DEMOCRACY is flourishing around the world, we Americans are having a hard time staying involved. Over the last thirty years, voter participation in the United States has decreased. Every day we hear that voters are angry, skeptical, and fatalistic about the political future of our country. The voting majority has in fact become the minority. As a result, more and more decisions are being made by a small number of voters who do not represent the diversity, needs, or interests of the populace.

Citizens who feel disenfranchised and turned off, mostly poor minorities and young persons, are joined by an increasingly skeptical middle class. All have one thing in common: a lost faith that each can make a difference. On this occasion of the 75th anniversary of woman suffrage in the United States, we must ask how is it that our democracy has lost so many voters in such a short time and what can we do to regain our belief? How do we remind ourselves of the struggle of women and minorities for the right to vote?

For most Americans, including African Americans, Latinos, women, and other groups historically discriminated against or excluded, involvement in our democratic form of government is a recent twentieth-century development. Efforts to expand and include all Americans in the political life of this country required a civil war and massive popular movements. The women's movement struggled for generations to win woman suffrage; it finally succeeded in 1920.

The civil rights efforts of the 1950s and 1960s along with action by the federal government brought about passage of the Voting Rights Act and other legislation that finally gave the African American and Latino communities the opportunity to engage in the political process. Although recent Supreme Court rulings significantly limited the force of the Voting Rights Act, be assured that political empowerment of African Americans and Latinos will continue, albeit at a much slower pace than before.

The National Voter Registration Act of 1993, better known as "Motor Voter," makes voter registration more accessible to citizens by allowing them to register at the same time they apply for drivers licenses. This act is increasing the numbers of voters in states with historically low voter registration numbers. Now that the mechanisms are in place, the challenge for us is to assure the public that it is worth their getting involved and that each individual can still make a difference.

For Latinos, the road to participation has been slow and marked with many detours. Many of the laws and practices such as poll taxes, purges, and intimidation that prevented African Americans from participating in the electoral process were also applied against Latinos. As recently as 1989, not a single Latino served on the Los Angeles County Board of Supervisors—this in a county where Latinos make up 40 percent of the population.

Additional barriers to participating in the political process exist for Latinos. We are a young community. Over 35 percent of our population is under the age of eighteen. The problem of our relative youth is compounded by the very low voter participation rate of young adults across the board: men and women, African Americans, whites, and Latinos. For older Latinos, language barriers have also hampered full participation. Another major impediment for Latinos is lack of citizenship. A significant percentage of the people in our community are legal residents but not yet citizens. Los Angeles County alone includes more than 1.8 million noncitizens who potentially are eligible for naturalization.

Notwithstanding these significant barriers, Latinos made great gains in the 1970s and 1980s. In the last three decades, the number of Latino elected officials has increased. In Texas alone, the change has been dramatic. The number of elected Latino officials in Texas grew from 367 in 1973 to 2,215 in 1995, including 455 women.

As we thrive on our victories that are moving us toward a better democracy, however, we must remind ourselves that to nurture and build on these gains we must learn from our past and seek better approaches.

PROPOSITION 187

On its face a vehicle for direct involvement in the democratic process, the initiative (the process of putting propositions on the ballot by means of voter petitions) has been used in California by those with resources and power to impose the views of the few upon the many.

Over the past twenty years, powerful forces have bypassed the legislative process and presented the electorate with myriad controversial, ill-crafted proposals involving complex and provocative issues. The weighing of interests that the legislative process in a democracy is intended to accomplish is ignored. Instead, negative, self-serving campaigns are waged that confuse the voters and appeal to their worst fears. Numerous initiatives have resulted in endless litigation, thereby abdicating the final decision to the courts, which in many instances are ill-suited to resolve society's problems.

Use of the initiative process to deal with contentious issues involving race, ethnicity, and language polarizes voters and frequently produces only superficial public debate; the results please few and leave many issues unanswered. Such was the impact of Proposition 187, the 1994 California initiative dealing with the status of immigrants.

Passed by 59 percent of California voters, Proposition 187 mandates the denial to undocumented immigrants of public education and social services such as health care. Proponents claim their objective is to drive the undocumented out of the country, yet neither the initiative nor the debate surrounding it dealt with the root causes of undocumented migration. Efforts to engage the public in an informed debate were futile in an election where the Republican candidates for governor and the U.S. Senate made passage of Proposition 187 their campaign centerpiece. Opponents of the initiative were underfunded and unable to get their message out to the voters.

The Latino community viewed passage of Proposition 187 as more than an effort to curtail undocumented immigration; its success represented a repudiation of our community by the electorate. For a community that has been struggling to incorporate itself into the mainstream of society, rejection by the voters was a heavy blow.

Since then many questions have been asked and many stories have been told about the circumstances surrounding the initiative. What lessons did we learn, and what good, if any, has come from the passage of Proposition 187?

When we in the Latino community learned that the initiative would qualify for the November 1994 ballot, we began to discuss how to mount a credible campaign against it. Those who spearheaded the effort to get the initiative on the ballot had the financial support of powerful Republican elected officials. That financial support was crucial. In order to gather enough signatures to qualify Proposition 187 for the ballot, paid signature gatherers were hired, further evidence that the initiative process is no longer a tool of the populace.

In California and other Western states where the initiative exists, the process has become a tool of powerful and special interests. The number of initiatives circulated, qualified, and adopted in California has now reached record proportions: a fivefold increase since 1960. According to a report of the California Commission on Campaign Financing, spending on initiatives has risen by as much as 1,200 percent since the early 1980s, peaking at $127 million in 1988.

An initial challenge for the opponents of Proposition 187 was the need to raise money. The consensus of the core group, spearheaded by Los Angeles County Supervisor Gloria Molina and State Senator Richard Polanco, was that Latinos would need $10 million to $15 million to mount a credible campaign.

For a community with very limited economic resources, a community that is considered powerless and ineffectual, the task was daunting and almost overwhelming. Moreover, California electoral campaigns are no longer conducted the old-fashioned way by directly approaching the voters. There are some thirty million residents in California, and television and radio, expensive vehicles for communicating, have now become the most effective means to reach this public.

Our first task was to organize our community and arrive at common principles upon which we all could agree. In 1993, the Mexican American Legal Defense Fund (MALDEF), with a long history of involvement in the immigration debate, took the first step in bringing together the Latino community. Out of a series of meetings, a group was formed, Proponents for Responsible Immigration Debate and Education (PRIDE).

PRIDE has these four principles at its core:

1. The right of citizenship by birth and through naturalization must not be forsaken or compromised, and naturalization must become a national priority.
2. Immigrants, including the undocumented, have basic human civil rights, including access to a public elementary and secondary education, emergency medical care, and health services.
3. The United States is entitled to control and regulate its borders, but border control must be civilian and guided by the values of efficiency, safety, dignity, and humanity.

4. The most effective means of reducing undocumented immigration is to raise the standard of living and improve life opportunities in the immigrants' countries of origin.

Our hope in putting forth these principles was to provide a basis for public debate and discussion. We understood that the principles are not in and of themselves solutions or answers to the many issues raised by immigration. But we argued that a more informed public discourse needed to take place. The debate had to start within the Latino community and branch out to the other communities.

Historically immigration and its implications have been a difficult issue for our community. Throughout the history of the United States, immigrants have been used as scapegoats when the economy soured or other social problems arose. The cyclical resurgence of these attitudes became apparent once again in the debate about Proposition 187. We believed that the consequences of the present anti-immigrant public hostility could be efforts to mass deport segments of our community. To illustrate that point during the campaign, we reprinted a 1931 headline from the *Los Angeles Times* that reads: "Ousting of Aliens Will Be Speeded."

Knowing that we could not raise the required amounts of money, we had to create a broad-based coalition of groups that could spread the word through their networks. We wanted to convene religious leaders, other ethnic immigrant communities, business groups, the League of Women Voters, unions, and other community groups that shared our concerns. The process of creating this coalition proved difficult and cumbersome. Groups that traditionally had supported our efforts refused to come on board.

Many feared the issue had become partisan and politicized and were concerned that their support might generate reprisals. Moral consciousness and leadership were sorely missing in this debate. Many others, such as members of the business community, remained neutral on the proposition, but supported the Republican candidates for governor and U.S. Senator, both of whom made immigration the "Willie Horton" issue of the day. Partisan efforts to use Proposition 187 as a tool to divide the public succeeded. As the debate became more divisive and ugly, our traditional allies were nowhere to be found.

Eventually Proposition 187 stimulated the formation of two major statewide political coalitions. The first was the political action committee Taxpayers Against Proposition 187, consisting of law enforcement organizations and officials, health care associations, social service providers, educational organizations including boards of education, religious leaders, and local elected officials. The other coalition, Californians United Against Proposition 187, received its thrust from immigrants rights advocates and organizations; eventually it became a multisector, multi-ethnic grassroots entity.

To educate and galvanize our base, the Latino community worked intensely with the Spanish-speaking press. The results were impressive. Latinos came out to vote in record numbers, but it was not enough. Even if every eligible Latino had voted, we still would have lost.

Nonetheless, those of us who are leaders in the Latino community realize that we must double our efforts to educate our community about the importance of voting and to demonstrate that Latinos did in fact make a difference. We also understand it is important to increase the number of voters through naturalization. These messages have been heard. Citizenship and naturalization as well as voter registration are now top agenda items of most Latino organizations. By the turn of the century, we hope to add an additional three million voters to the rolls.

Even though we learned some hard lessons, not all was lost. Some very courageous public voices came to our defense. Former Housing and Urban Development secretary Jack Kemp and former Education secretary William Bennett, both Republicans, spoke forcefully against the proposition.

Unfortunately we could not get the information out quickly enough to the public. The Catholic church and other religious groups took the message to their constituents, for example, but the flocks did not follow their religious leaders. This pattern also was seen with many other interest groups. Although group leaders understood the danger of

Proposition 187 and worked to defeat it, they could not deliver their constituents.

THE AFTERMATH

The passage of Proposition 187 sent a loud message to the Latino community: we must become involved and have our voices heard. The impact of Proposition 187 has yet to be felt. The day after its passage, MALDEF and four other groups filed lawsuits in federal and state courts. The federal lawsuit, *Gregorio T. v. Wilson,* challenges all provisions of the initiative as an unconstitutional usurpation of the federal government's exclusive power to regulate immigration. The suit also contends that Proposition 187 violates the equal protection and due process guarantees under the U.S. Constitution. The state court action, *Jesus Doe* v. *Regents of the University of California,* raises state and federal constitutional and statutory claims, including a claim under the Family Educational Rights and Privacy Act. As with so many other initiatives, the outcome now rests with the courts; ultimately the U.S. Supreme Court will need to resolve this debate.

In the meantime, Latinos have learned a painful but valuable lesson: the future of this country and its democracy rests with citizen involvement. We must get involved. We have learned that democracy can be oppressive and dictatorial if all of its citizens do not participate.

This country is undergoing a profound and permanent change. Its demographics are changing. It is becoming more diverse. Its economy is transforming itself into an internationally interdependent information and service world economy without borders. California's future, tied to the Americas and the Pacific Rim, is in the vanguard of this change.

Latinos are poised to bridge this transformation and to infuse this democracy with new vigor and life. For the Latino community, Proposition 187 was a cruel teacher. But as astute students, we will put the lesson to good use.

FOR THE
NEXT
GENERATION

Hillary Rodham Clinton is first lady of the United States. A graduate of Wellesley College and Yale Law School, she became a staff attorney for the Children's Defense Fund in 1973. A year later, she joined the impeachment inquiry staff of the Judiciary Committee of the U.S. House of Representatives to work on the Watergate impeachment proceedings. Following her marriage, she taught on the law faculty of the University of Arkansas at Fayetteville. As first lady of Arkansas for twelve years, she continued her advocacy on behalf of children and families and also worked full-time as a partner in a law firm. She has served on several boards of directors, including the Children's Defense Fund, Child Care Action Campaign, Children's TV Workshop, and the Eleanor Roosevelt Institute.

A Call to Action

HILLARY RODHAM CLINTON

THIS IMPORTANT GATHERING of the world's women at the United Nations Fourth World Conference on Women in Beijing is a celebration—a celebration of the contributions women make in every aspect of life: in the home, on the job, in the community, as mothers, wives, sisters, daughters, learners, workers, citizens, and leaders.

It is also a coming together, much in the way women come together every day in every country. We come together in fields and in factories, in village markets and supermarkets, in living rooms and boardrooms. Whether it is while playing with our children in the park or washing clothes in a river or taking a break at the office watercooler, we come

---

Note: Adapted from remarks to the United Nations Fourth World Conference on Women, Beijing, China, September 5, 1995.

together and talk about our aspirations and concerns. And time and time again, our talk turns to our children and our families.

However different we may appear, there is far more that unites us than divides us. We share a common future. And we seek common ground so that we may bring new dignity and respect to women and girls all over the world—and in so doing, bring new strength and stability to families as well.

By gathering in Beijing in 1995, we focus world attention on the issues that matter most in the lives of women and their families; access to education, health care, jobs, and credit and the chance to enjoy basic legal and human rights and to participate fully in the political life of their countries.

There are some who criticize the United Nations for convening the Fourth World Conference on Women. Let them listen to the voices of women in their homes, neighborhoods, and workplaces. There are some who wonder whether the lives of women and girls matter to economic and political progress around the globe. Let them look at the women going about their daily lives: the homemakers, nurses, teachers, lawyers, policy makers, and women who run their own businesses.

A World Conference on Women compels governments and people everywhere to listen, look, and face the world's most pressing problems. Wasn't it after the 1985 Third World Conference on Women in Nairobi that the world focused for the first time on the crisis of domestic violence?

What we are learning around the world is that if women are healthy and educated, their families will flourish. If women are free from violence, their families will flourish. If women have a chance to work and earn as full and equal partners in society, their families will flourish. And when families flourish, communities and nations will flourish. That is why every woman, every man, every child, every family, and every nation on our planet has a stake in the discussion that took place at the conference in Beijing.

Over the past twenty-five years, I have worked persistently on issues relating to women, children, and families. And as first lady, I have had the opportunity to learn even more about the challenges facing women in my own country and around the world.

I have met new mothers in Indonesia who come together regularly in their village to discuss nutrition, family planning, and baby care. I have met working parents in Denmark who talk about the comfort they feel in knowing that their children can be cared for in creative, safe, and nurturing after-school centers. I have met women in South Africa who helped lead the struggle to end apartheid and are now helping to build a new democracy. I have met with leading women of my own hemisphere who are working every day to promote literacy and better health care for the children in their countries. I have met women in India and Bangladesh who are taking out small loans to buy milk cows, rickshaws, thread, and other materials to create livelihoods for themselves and their families. I have met doctors and nurses in Belarus and Ukraine who are trying to keep children alive in the aftermath of Chernobyl.

One of our great challenges is to give voice to women everywhere whose experiences go unnoticed, whose words go unheard.

Women make up more than half the world's population. Women are 70 percent of the world's poor and two-thirds of those who are not taught to read and write. Women are the primary caretakers for most of the world's children and elderly. Yet much of the work women do is not valued—not by economists, not by historians, not by popular culture, not by government leaders.

At this very moment, women around the world are giving birth, raising children, cooking meals, washing clothes, cleaning houses, planting crops, working on assembly lines, running companies, and running countries. But women also are dying from diseases that should have been prevented or treated; they are watching their children succumb to malnutrition caused by poverty and economic deprivation; they are being denied the right to go to school by their own fathers and brothers; they are being forced into prostitution; and they are being barred from the bank lending office and banned from the ballot box.

Those of us who have the opportunity to speak out, have a responsibility to speak up for those women whose voices cannot be heard. As an American, I want to speak up for women in my own country—women who are raising children on the minimum wage, women who can't afford health care or child care, women whose lives are threatened by violence, including violence in their own homes.

I want to speak up for mothers who are fighting for good schools, safe neighborhoods, clean air, and clean airwaves; for older women, some of them widows, who have raised their families and are now finding that their skills and life experiences are not valued in the workplace; for women who are working all night as nurses, hotel clerks, and fast-food chefs so that they can be at home during the day with their kids; and for women everywhere who simply don't have time to do everything they are called upon to do each day.

I want to speak for them and for women around the world who are denied the chance to go to school, or see a doctor, or own property, or have a say about the direction of their lives simply because they are women.

The truth is that most women around the world work both inside and outside the home, usually by necessity. We need to understand that there is no formula for how women should lead their lives. That is why we must respect the choices that each woman makes for herself and her family. Every woman deserves the chance to realize her God-given potential. We also must recognize that women will never gain full dignity until their human rights are respected and protected. The goals of the United Nations Fourth World Conference on Women—to strengthen families and societies by empowering women to take greater control over their own destinies—cannot be fully achieved unless all governments accept their responsibility to protect and promote internationally recognized human rights.

The international community has long acknowledged that both women and men are entitled to a range of protections and personal freedoms, from the right of personal security to the right to determine freely the number and spacing of the children they bear. No one should be forced to remain silent for fear of religious or political persecution, arrest, abuse, or torture.

Tragically women are most often the ones whose human rights are violated. Even in the late twentieth century, the rape of women continues to be used as an instrument of armed conflict. Women and children make up a large majority of the world's refugees. And when women are excluded from the political process, they become even more vulnerable to abuse.

On this eve of a new millennium, I believe that it is time to break our silence. It is time for the world to understand that we no longer find it acceptable to discuss women's rights as separate from human rights.

Abuses against women have continued because, for too long, the history of women has been a history of silence. Even today there are those who are trying to silence our words.

Our voices must be heard loud and clear:

It is a violation of *human* rights when babies are denied food, drowned, or suffocated or have their spines broken simply because they are born girls.

It is a violation of *human* rights when women and girls are sold into slavery or prostitution.

It is a violation of *human* rights when women are doused with gasoline, set on fire, and burned to death because their marriage dowries are deemed too small.

It is a violation of *human* rights when individual women are raped in their own communities and when thousands of women are subjected to rape as a tactic or prize of war.

It is a violation of *human* rights when a leading cause of death worldwide among women ages fourteen to forty-four is the violence they are subjected to in their own homes by their own relatives.

It is a violation of *human* rights when young girls are brutalized by the painful and degrading practice of genital mutilation.

It is a violation of *human* rights when women are denied the right to plan their own families, and that includes being forced to have abortions or being sterilized against their will.

If there is one message that echoes forth as a result of the Beijing Conference, let it be that human rights are women's rights and women's rights are human rights.

Let us not forget that among those rights are the right to speak freely—and the right to be heard. Women must enjoy the right to participate fully in the social and political lives of their countries if we want freedom and democracy to thrive and endure. Freedom means the right of people to assemble, organize, and debate openly. It means respecting the views of those who may disagree with the views of their governments. It means not taking citizens away from their loved ones and jailing them, mistreating them, or denying them their freedom or dignity because of their peaceful expression of their ideas and opinions.

In 1995, America celebrated the 75th anniversary of woman suffrage. It took almost 150 years after the signing of our Declaration of Independence for American women to win the right to vote. It took 72 years of organized struggle on the part of many courageous women and men for women to finally win the right to vote. It was one of America's most divisive philosophical wars. But it was also a bloodless war. Woman suffrage was achieved without a shot being fired.

In 1995, America also observed the 50th anniversary of the end of World War II. We were reminded of the good that comes when men and women join together to combat the forces of tyranny and build a better world. We have seen peace prevail in most places for a half century. We have avoided another world war.

But we have not solved older, deeply rooted problems that continue to diminish the potential of half the world's population. Now it is time to act on behalf of women everywhere. If we take bold steps to better the lives of women, we will be taking bold steps to better the lives of children and families, too. Families rely on mothers and wives for emotional support and care; families rely on women for labor in the home; and increasingly families rely on women for the income needed to raise healthy children and care for other relatives. Yet as long as discrimination and inequities remain commonplace everywhere in the world—as long as girls and women are valued less, fed less, fed last, overworked, underpaid, not schooled, and subjected to violence in and out of their homes—the potential of the human family to create a peaceful, prosperous world will not be realized.

All of us must participate in a conversation about how to shape the changes we seek in the world we share. Too often a deafening silence still sounds when women's concerns and women's voices are raised. We must move beyond rhetoric, beyond recognition of problems, to working together, to joining in common efforts to build that common ground we hope to see.

We must call the world to action. We must heed that call so that we can create a world in which every woman is treated with respect and dignity, every boy and girl is loved and cared for equally, and every family has the hope of a strong and stable future.

That is the work before us. That is the work before *all* of us who have a vision of the world we want to see for our children and our grandchildren. The time is now.

WILMA P. MANKILLER was principal chief of the Cherokee Nation from 1985 to 1995 and deputy principal chief from 1983 to 1985. She is a trustee of the Ford Foundation, Citizens Trust Holdings, and the Freedom Forum and past president of the Inter-Tribal Council of Five Tribes and the Arkansas Riverbed Authority. She previously served on the boards of the Ms. Foundation for Women, Indian Law Resource Center, Seventh Generation Fund, Rainbow Television Workshop, Oklahoma Academy for State Goals, and Oklahoma Indian Affairs Commission. She is the author of *Mankiller: A Chief and Her People* (1993) and coeditor of the forthcoming *Reader's Companion to the History of Women in the U.S.* She holds a B.S. degree in social science and nine honorary doctorates.

Entering the Twenty-First Century— On Our Own Terms

WILMA P. MANKILLER

I N THE OLD DAYS, the Cherokee people believed that the world existed in a precarious balance, and only right or correct actions kept it from tumbling. Wrong actions were believed to disturb the balance. An important part of the balance was harmony and equality between men and women. Cherokee government once was described as "petticoat government" because of the strong influence of women.

Cherokee assimilation into the culture and values of the larger society eventually forced Cherokee women into a secondary role. Despite all the intermarriage and adaptation to non-Cherokee culture, however, Cherokee women still had the right to vote long before it was granted to American women. Unfortunately, by the time I ran in my first election for deputy chief in 1983, our history of balance between men and women seemed to be long forgotten.

As they approach the twenty-first century, Americans have a woeful lack of accurate information, either historical or contemporary, about Native American people. Most Americans are left to fill this void with negative stereotypes from old Western movies or romanticized paintings and collections in museums. A friend of mine, a Seneca scholar, once remarked that many people have a mental snapshot of Native people taken three hundred years ago and they want to retain that image.

THE TRAIL OF TEARS

The question I am asked most frequently is this: "Why do tribal governments even exist, and what are your educational needs as you redevelop and revitalize tribal communities?"

Today many Americans look at the data relative to Native people and ask: How did these people get into this situation? What happened? Why do they have the highest infant mortality rate, the worst housing rate, the highest unemployment rate? What went wrong? It is difficult to understand our contemporary problems without knowing something about our history and all the external factors that played a part in where we are today.

Throughout the Americas, tribal governments have existed in one form or another since time immemorial. Few Americans understand that the history of the Americas is really the history of Native people. When the colonists began forming what ultimately became the United States, tribal communities were dealt with on a nation-to-nation basis, and sometimes treaties were struck between the Indian nations and the newly emerging America. The nation-to-nation relationship between tribes and the U.S. government continues to exist.

So today, when you hear people talking about treaty rights, what they are talking about are agreements made between two nations, most of them made before 1868. Now some people will say that the validity of those treaties is in question because of their age. Well, that makes no sense at all. Many significant world documents exist that are as old or older than many of these Indian treaties. Just look at the U.S. Constitution and Bill of Rights, for example. Their age doesn't make them invalid.

The story of the Cherokee Nation is strikingly similar to the story of every Native community in this country. Prior to the early nineteenth century, the Cherokee people lived in the Southeastern part of the United States, in what is now the general area of Georgia, South Carolina, North Carolina, and Tennessee. For the most part, we were agricultural people. Our contact with Europeans came fairly early, in the late sixteenth century. We adapted or adopted some of their tools and, as a result of this contact, became somewhat acculturated. As time went on, we became interested in sending some of our people to colonial educational institutions.

As a policy, our tribal leaders tried to get along with their southern neighbors and with this newly emerging country. In fact, at one time, we fought alongside Andrew Jackson against the Creeks. From my reading of history, I think our leaders felt that if we could endear ourselves to General Jackson, who later became president, the Cherokees would receive better and fairer treatment. But it didn't work.

By the time General Jackson became President Jackson, he fully supported moving the entire body of the Cherokee Nation to Indian Territory, to what is now Oklahoma. Many non-Indians supported our opposition to this move. Among them were several very prominent and active missionaries—people who today would be called pacifists or zealots—who actually went to jail fighting for our right to remain in our ancestral Cherokee homeland.

Our chief at the time, John Ross, was a progressive individual who believed in the American judicial system. He encouraged making the argument for protection of the Cherokee Nation in the courts. When the United States Supreme Court sided with the Cherokees in one case, President Jackson's response was to ignore the decision. And talk of removal continued. Jackson pushed for the Indian Removal Act, which passed—by just one vote.

As removal became more and more imminent, bitter internal divisions erupted within our tribe. Part of our people wanted to stay in the Southeast and fight to the death for the right to remain in our homeland. Another part of our people felt we should move peacefully to Indian Territory, resettle and rebuild communities there.

Despite our best efforts, removal did occur. In 1838, the United States Army, about 3,000 troops, began rounding up our ancestors, inventorying their property, and placing them in what were euphemistically called stockades. Today the stockades would more properly be called concentration camps. Our people were imprisoned in the stockades and prepared for removal to Indian Territory.

The forced removal by the United States Army occurred throughout 1838 and up until April 1839. Among the approximately 17,000 Cherokees were hundreds of free African Americans and slaves. By the time the last contingent of Cherokees arrived in Indian Territory, roughly one-fourth of our tribe had died while prisoners in the stockades or on the forced march through several states.

Because of the large loss of lives, the removal became known as the Trail of Tears. It was one of the most terrible things that ever happened to our people.

REBUILDING A NATION

What happened after April of 1839 is truly remarkable. When the Cherokees arrived in Indian Territory, everything had been torn apart—our families, our political system, and our cultural system. Our social structure had been left behind, and we were in a new geographic area. Our people assessed the situation and began to build the community, their families, and the tribe.

We built a judicial system and, most important, an educational system. By the mid 1840s, we were printing a newspaper published in Cherokee and in English. We established a capital at Cherokee Nation and built beautiful institutions of government, which still stand today as the oldest buildings in what is now Oklahoma. During this period, when we had control over our own lives, we experienced a golden era of the Cherokee Nation. We were more literate than the neighboring non-Indian population.

In looking at some old papers, I discovered that even in the 1840s, there were some people in this country who were still questioning whether or not Indians were human beings or whether Indians had souls. And while this debate was going on among this small circle of people, we were running our own educational systems and operating a highly sophisticated tribal government.

We continued to rebuild ourselves as a nation and also to rebuild our families and communities. Then the Civil War came, dividing the entire country. When the United States began to come back together again after the Civil War, its leaders started talking about opening Indian Territory to non-Indian settlements, something we had been told they would never do. When the Cherokees were removed to Indian Territory, we not only lost many lives, we also gave up thousands of acres of land, in fact much of the Southeast. We were told that, in exchange for all that, we would be able to live in Indian Territory, now eastern Oklahoma, uninterrupted forever. But as happened not only with our tribe but with many other tribes, those promises were ignored. History began to repeat itself.

In 1906, when Oklahoma became a state, our central tribal government was abolished. Our judicial system was stopped; our school system was closed. Most important to us as a people, land we had held in common was divided into allotments for individual tribal members. I think that act had more impact on our internal social system than any other single event at the turn of the twentieth century.

From 1906 to 1971, we fell into terrible decline. By the time we began to rebuild, in 1971, we had one of the lowest educational attainment levels of any group in Oklahoma, high infant mortality, and numerous other social indicators of decline. Many of our people were living without the basic amenities that every American should have.

A strange thing happened to our view of leadership during that period; it became a concept that was external to us and our communities.

The president of the United States appointed our leaders, who tended to come from wealthy or prominent families. People perceived that leadership was something only prominent wealthy members of our tribe could aspire to. When in 1971 we were permitted once again to elect our own leaders, we followed the same pattern.

Our first elected chief was a Cherokee fellow, William W. Keeler, who was chairman of the board of Phillips Petroleum. He was followed in 1975 by Ross Swimmer, who was president of a bank, a lawyer, and of course, an Indian chief.

When Bill Keeler began revitalizing the Cherokee Nation in 1971, which was a dream of his, he started in a storefront in Tahlequah, Oklahoma. We were without funds at the time. Most people say that Bill Keeler managed Phillips Petroleum with his head and managed the Cherokee Nation with his heart. I think this may be true.

When I walked in the door of the Cherokee Nation tribal offices in September of 1977 looking for a job, I never dreamed that one day I would have the honor and privilege of leading the second largest tribe in North America. My primary focus was on obtaining a position that would allow me to support my two children and make a contribution to the community. At that time, there were no female executives; there had never been a female deputy chief or a female principal chief. No one would have predicted that my first job at the Cherokee Nation would lead steadily to my eventual election as the first female deputy chief in 1983 and then as the first female principal chief in 1987 and again in 1991.

In the past quarter century, we have made incredible strides. All the development that occurred took place because of our own hard work. Unlike some tribes, we had no marketable natural resources or any other kind of leg up. We just had our own determination to, once again, rebuild a tribal community and a tribal government.

Today we are the largest tribe in Oklahoma, with 175,000 registered tribal members and thousands more who are not registered. The Cherokee Nation, our homeland now, is in the eastern part of Oklahoma, covering all or part of fourteen counties and having borders with Arkansas and Missouri and Kansas.

We are a significant employer in eastern Oklahoma. We operate six primary health care clinics, Head Start programs, a boarding school, a fully accredited high school, and a Job Corps center that provides vocational education not only for Cherokee and other Indian students but also for all students seeking such training. We build houses and water systems, provide basic social services, job training, and literacy education. We own a number of businesses and generate a significant amount of our own income. Our flagship business is Cherokee Nation Industries; it has succeeded for a quarter century, which makes us all very happy.

EDUCATION: A CHEROKEE IDEAL

The history of Cherokee involvement in education tends to dispel negative stereotypes about Native people. Because of our early European contact in the Southeast, some of our members began to take part in the educational system of the Western world. Tribal officials felt it was necessary for some of our people to obtain a formal Western education in order to deal more effectively with the emerging United States government.

After our removal to Indian Territory, not only did we build the first educational system, Indian or non-Indian, west of the Mississippi but we also, most significantly, decided to educate women, a radical idea for our part of the world at the time. Possessed with little knowledge about how to administer an educational system for women, tribal officials sent an emissary to Mt. Holyoke College to enlist aid in establishing the Cherokee Female Seminary. With the assistance of several dedicated women from Mt. Holyoke, the Cherokee Female Seminary flourished until Oklahoma statehood. The course of study was so advanced that some educators compared the Cherokee Female Seminary diploma to the equivalent of two years of college.

The best argument possible for continued support of tribal governments is to compare where our people were when we had some real control over our own destiny and what happened to us when there was a strong attempt to abolish our government.

When Oklahoma became a state and the Cherokee central tribal government was thrown into disarray, the schools were closed. It was over the next sixty years that the Cherokee people went from being relatively literate to having one of the lowest educational attainment levels in Oklahoma. As the Cherokee Nation began an intense period of revitalization in 1971, education became a top priority. After nearly a quarter century, we are finally beginning to see overall improvement in the educational attainment level of the Cherokee people. Every year we provide about $800,000 in higher education scholarships, primarily to undergraduates, giving a much smaller amount to graduate students.

We cannot, however, undertake the task of education alone. More support must be given to such programs as Head Start and programs that offer after-school tutorial assistance, bilingual education, strong counseling, student and family support services, and college-level financial aid. The Women, Infants, and Children program (WIC), as much as any other support service, has probably contributed more to higher education than we will ever know.

In general, the educational attainment level for Native students in America is still alarmingly low. For the most part, Native students attend school in poverty areas, where the school systems are severely underfunded. Moreover, all too often these children are denied an existence as members of a distinct cultural group.

The more traditional Native students come from families where education is viewed quite differently than it is by Western society. In these families, the value of a formal education is not measured solely by personal, professional, or economic goals. Instead, children are taught that everything is interconnected to form a whole. Spirituality, for example, is not something one expresses once a week by dressing up and attending Sunday morning services. Rather, spiritual values are incorporated into all aspects of daily life.

The same holds true in education. Education in some tribal communities need not take place only while students sit in a classroom memorizing specific facts. Education also occurs at ceremonial grounds where tribal people of all ages participate in practices that have been part of the community since time immemorial. There is a great sense of interdependence among Native people. Grandparents and extended family members live either in multigenerational households or close to one another. Family members pass on stories that may have a deceptively simple plot but that always express a value or moral to be learned. Education is an ongoing lifetime process that exists not in a vacuum, but as part of the whole.

In many Native communities, a much greater emphasis is placed on the collective achievements of the family or the community than on individual achievements. Native people who achieve great personal success, though respected, are not held in the same esteem as those who achieve great success for others. You could do some great thing, make a million dollars, and personally accomplish a great deal yet not be held in as high esteem as if you had served others.

When students are brought up in this kind of environment and enter an institution of higher learning where the values are very different, they sometimes falter and think there is something wrong with them. For example, a Cherokee fellow who went to Harvard Medical School began to call home all the time because he thought there was something wrong with him. He wanted to be a doctor in an Indian Health Service clinic, but his classmates thought he was out of his mind; they had career goals involving prestige and financial rewards. Not everyone is like this young man, but value systems like his tend to exist in the communities where people remain close to cultural values.

What does this mean for college counselors and others who want to help Native students obtain a college education? At a minimum, it means having an open attitude and listening to the unique needs of each

Native student. Her or his historical background and culture should be understood or at least respected, with an awareness that there is no Native culture per se in this country but more than 400 different tribal groups, each with a distinct history, culture, and language.

We look into the faces of our young Native people and see, despite everything, hope. We must keep that hope alive by doing all we can to help them obtain the kind of education that is necessary for survival in a highly technological world. What tribal people most need today, as we continue to dig our way out of the devastation of the past two hundred years, is a cadre of well-trained young people to help us enter the twenty-first century on our own terms.

ENTERING THE TWENTY-FIRST CENTURY

A co-worker once described me as someone who likes to dance along the edge of the roof. I never have figured out whether that means I am self-confident or just impulsive. Either way, I definitely was out on the edge when I decided to seek elective office as deputy principal chief in 1983.

Neither that first election nor any of my subsequent elections has been easy. Tribal politics, even in the best of circumstances, are more personal and bruising than mainstream elective politics, probably because the electorate is more like family. Being a female made all my elections even more difficult.

Gender-based opposition to female leaders is hard to deal with because it comes from the wholly irrational idea that women are unsuited for leadership. How does one deal with such foolish ideas? During my first election, I read a saying (on the back of a tea box!): "Don't ever argue with a fool because someone walking by won't be able to tell which one is a fool." That little piece of wisdom helped me enormously as I went through an election where my candidacy was sometimes ridiculed by my own people.

After winning election in 1983, my leadership style, which has been described as collaborative and understated, was initially mistaken for weakness. I experienced enormous stress because I felt I was being held to a different standard than my male predecessor. I kept longer hours, worked harder, and believed, rightly or wrongly, that if I failed, I would be failing other women who might follow me.

Today an increasing number of women hold tribal leadership positions throughout Indian country, but we still have a long way to go before we reach equity in elective politics, in tribal governments, or in society in general.

Women who are successful in local, tribal, state, and federal elections generally must have résumés twice as long as those of their male opponents. It continues to be very tough to attract the money necessary to wage a political campaign and deal with opposition to female leadership. As a woman in Memphis once said to me: "We will have equity in elective politics when we can elect mediocre women to high office in this country."

Until then, let us draw renewed inspiration from the women who fought so hard for our right to vote. Let us continue working to elect women at every level of government. As we approach the twenty-first century, those women will join us in fighting racial intolerance, halting the attack on poor women and women on welfare, and eliminating bias against aging women and women with disabilities.

Several years ago, after I presented a lecture in a Midwestern city, a Native man approached me with an important message. He had heard a prophecy that this particular time period is the time of women—a time for women to assume a more important role in society. He described it as "the time of the butterfly." Perhaps so.

Perhaps the time has finally come for the balance between male and female leadership to be restored.

CONDOLEEZZA RICE is provost and professor of political science at Stanford University. Formerly she was a Hoover Institution Fellow, a senior fellow at the Institute for International Studies, and a member of the Center for International Security and Arms Control. From 1989 to 1991, Rice was special assistant to the president for National Security Affairs and also senior director for Soviet and East European Affairs at the National Security Council. She is the author of *Uncertain Allegiance: The Soviet Union and the Czechoslovak Army* (1984), *The Gorbachev Era* (with Alexander Dallin, 1986), and *Germany Unified and Europe Transformed* (with Philip Zelikov, 1995). She received a B.A. degree from the University of Denver, an M.A. degree from the University of Notre Dame, and a Ph.D. degree from the University of Denver Graduate School of International Studies.

Small Steps, Giant Leaps

CONDOLEEZZA RICE

*I*N THE LAST DECADE of the twentieth century, at a time of a great
and challenging transitions, many images of change elicit hope.
Who can forget the pictures of German meeting German across the no-
man's land that had been the Berlin Wall? Who can forget the celebration of democracy's dawn in Poland or the "velvet revolution" in
Czechoslovakia? Who can forget the pictures of the old and sick in
South Africa voting for the first time—voting with enthusiasm and
pride for a better future they personally will never see? And who can
forget the peaceful death of the Soviet Union as, on Christmas night in
1991, the hammer and sickle of the mighty empire came down from
atop the Kremlin for the last time?

While we cannot forget these images, they are surely fading, giving way to a kind of quiet despair about the difficult work yet to be done at home, work on democracy in America. It is fitting that we have turned inward to look at ourselves. There is much at stake, here and abroad, because people still look to America to see whether a multi-ethnic democracy can work.

Like most Americans, I listened with some skepticism to the Cold War claim that America was a "beacon of democracy." When American presidents said that, I chalked it up to bad speechwriting and hyperbole. Sometimes I was just plain embarrassed, because America is at best an imperfect democracy. It was imperfect at its birth. When the founding fathers said, "We the people," they did not mean me. My ancestors were property—a fraction of a man. Women were not included in those immortal constitutional phrases concerning the right of the people, "in the course of human events," to choose who would rule.

Yet, as I traveled in Eastern Europe and the Soviet Union in 1989 and 1990 as the grip of their totalitarian governments was slipping, I understood for the first time that the claim was true. I saw America reflected through the eyes of those still searching for the simple rights that we take for granted: the right to say what we think, to worship freely, to choose those who are to rule. I came to see democracy not as a finished product but as a work in progress. The hard work begins again each day, whether in a mature country like our own or in the emerging democracies abroad.

REDEFINING HORIZONS

In this respect, America's progress toward the inclusion of more and more of us in "We the people" takes on new meaning. Progress comes step by step and sometimes seems painfully slow. But that should not obscure the fact that those small steps add up to giant leaps. Nowhere is this more evident than in the changing role of women in America.

And no institution has been more important in fostering those changes than higher education.

Women have enrolled in universities in vastly larger numbers than ever before and have expanded their presence into every conceivable field. There is no better place in the world than America and no better time in history than today to be a young woman standing at the dawn of one's professional life. The young college women of today will have choices, opportunities, and responsibilities that could not have been imagined even half a century ago.

Stanford has always admitted women, and that birthmark of co-education remains an important and defining characteristic of the university. But even at Stanford, where women have always been present, a great deal has changed. David Starr Jordan, the first president of Stanford, had said that "women and men will be admitted on identical terms." When the first class enrolled at Stanford in 1891, 142 (25.4 percent) of the 559 students were women. However, as the percentage of women grew to 40 percent in 1898 and Jane Lathrop Stanford feared that the university established in memory of her only son was becoming a "woman's college," the enrollment of women was restricted to 500, a number that remained in effect until the 1930s.

Although David Starr Jordan supported higher education for women, he echoed the popular belief "that a woman naturally would prefer those subjects and activities suited to her sex." While there would always be the exceptional woman, ready and able to compete in a man's profession, in general, he noted, "Women take up higher education because they enjoy it, men because their careers depend upon it."

One wonders what the founders of Stanford would think today. The 1995 entering class was more than 50 percent women for the first time in the university's history. And what of "those subjects . . . suited to her sex?" The Stanford women who have gone on to the U.S. Senate, the U.S. Supreme Court, space flight, the fighter pilot corps, and other such "suitable" endeavors have simply redefined the boundaries of the acceptable and the expected.

This is true, of course, not just for Stanford women. Higher education permits us to break boundaries and to recast ourselves. It is one of the few truly transforming experiences in America today. It matters not whether we are poor or rich, minority or majority, urban or rural, foreign or American—a college education forces us to stretch our imaginations and redefine our horizons. When universities are most successful, they provide the environment and support for students to learn what they are good at doing and what they do less well. If a student is lucky, she will find a passion—an interest so powerful that it can sustain her throughout life.

FINDING A PASSION

Early in my undergraduate career, I considered myself destined to be a concert musician. I could read music before I could read words. But in college, I met real musical prodigies. I had to face the fact that I was a good musician but not a great one.

As a junior in college in search of a major, I was lucky enough, instead, to find a passion: I found the Soviet Union and Russia. I was mostly drawn to the study of the Soviet military establishment—hardcore bombs and bullets. While I found the history of war horrific, I also found that I wanted to know more, and so I studied and learned to think about the unthinkable—nuclear war and how to prevent it.

When I started down that road, it did not occur to me that I was outside the boundaries of what a black woman should want to know. I simply found the issues and the concerns riveting. When the opportunity came to serve President Bush in the White House during the extraordinary years that ended the Cold War, I was grateful that I had followed my passion, not that which had been defined for me.

American women have no reason to do anything but follow their passions. Barriers are insurmountable only if we see them as such. And while it is important to have role models, people who can show us the way to success, there is no reason to believe that role models need to look like us to show us the path to success in a particular career. Were that the case, there would be no firsts—no first woman on the Supreme Court, no first woman in space. It is not that racism or sexism have been eradicated or that they will never rear up before us. But to be deterred by them in the abstract, before we try pushing and shoving at the door we find closed to us, is to give them a victory that they might otherwise not win.

I will admit that I had two important advantages growing up that may well explain this view. First, I was born in segregated Birmingham, Alabama, in 1954. What was the advantage? My parents were extraordinary enough to convince me that though I could not have a hamburger at the Woolworth's lunch counter, I could be president of the United States if I wanted to be. In short, they did not allow me to believe in obstacles. Second, they gave me a strong grounding in religious faith—an asset for which there is no substitute when reason and intellect fail to explain why.

There is a third advantage I have that is common to the women of America and that is the very character of this country. The people of Eastern Europe, the former Soviet Union, South Africa, and many other lands are affirming a set of values that are at the very heart of America at its best. They are saying that the individual, not the state, is the locomotive of human history, that all people are created equal, and that out of the darkest past can emerge a bright future.

MOVING FORWARD

At this time of the affirmation of our values, we Americans are uncertain, frightened, and pessimistic about what lies ahead. Pessimism is, in and of itself, the greatest impediment to making things better. Pessimism gets in the way of the belief that individuals working hard, step by step, bring about change. That belief is the most American of values. It was the spirit of America's founding fathers who left Europe and built a new system of governance in a faraway place. It was the spirit that emboldened men and women to go West, hoping to find opportunity. It was the spirit that sustained my ancestors, the slaves, to believe that somehow, some way, there would be a better day.

We desperately need to rekindle that spirit in America. Every American bears responsibility for helping to bring it back. But we cannot do that if we are too focused on the barriers to our own advancement and if we become bitter and encumbered—unable to turn to the needs of those for whom America is truly still without promise.

Put simply, America is a fragile but great experiment. It is built on the belief that *many can become one.* At a time when peoples across the world seem intent on ever finer distinctions between "we" and "they" and when difference can be a license to kill, that is a remarkable statement. We have made great strides in giving meaning to our founding fathers' statement, "We the people." Rather than condemn our imperfect democracy by concentrating on its past, we need to turn to the future and the hard work of moving forward.

Those of us who have benefited from the transforming nature of higher education have a particular responsibility to that cause. We have been so lucky, allowed to find what we do well and to pursue it without fear of persecution for our ideas or our views.

And those of us who are women and minorities owe a special debt to those who pushed and shoved at closed doors so that opportunity would be ours. To ignore the hard work still to be done in that regard would be foolhardy. But to pretend that little has been achieved, to assume that insurmountable barriers still stand in the way, is to diminish what those great pioneers achieved. That would be a great tragedy, for while our democratic journey as Americans is not complete, we are still very much farther down the road than those in many places who now look to us for confirmation that it is a road worth taking.

MARIA LUISA MERCADO is an attorney in Galveston, Texas.
Appointed to the board of the Legal Services Corporation in
1993, she was a staff attorney for West Texas Legal Services
(1981–1983), and an assistant attorney general of Texas
(1983–1989). A cofounder and first state president of the Hispanic Women's Network of Texas, she served on the Governor's
Commission for Women and Leadership Texas. She is a former
vice chair and board member of the Mexican American Legal
Defense and Education Fund and was elected president of the
national Housing Assistance Council in 1995. Born in Mexico,
Mercado became an American citizen on July 21, 1976. She is
a graduate of West Texas State University and Antioch School
of Law.

My Daughter's Generation

MARIA LUISA MERCADO

M Y PARENTS WERE immigrant Mexican farmworkers who never voted in an election in this country, and my nine-year-old daughter talks of being president one day.

There is a lot of hope in our family; however, I can't help but remember the past. I look around the country today and wonder and worry about how easily my daughter's dream might be destroyed. From time to time, I have considered what I would want my daughter to think about if I were not around to advise her before her first political race. I am sure I would want her to know that change in this country came after a lot of struggle and heartbreak.

When American women gained the precious right to vote in 1920, some people believed the last vestige of legal discrimination that barred participation in our democracy had been eliminated. With that barrier removed, they thought, injustice and all remaining forms of discrimination would soon end. After all, women were the majority, and the ballot box would cure all the problems. We all know that did not happen.

While the right to vote was a step on the path to full participation for women in our society, it was not the end of the road. Women and minorities still need real access to the decision makers, and they need to become decision makers themselves. All our daughters must do more than simply cast an educated vote if they want to become full participants in this society.

We must educate our daughters (and their brothers) about the past. We must teach them to be thoughtful about power and democracy in America as they proceed with their political lives. Like many of us, I have tried to explain things to my daughter by telling her stories about her family. History is easier to remember when it is personalized. She knows about my parents coming to this country from Mexico when I was a child and the constant struggle of my parents and seven surviving brothers and sisters to make a living by working in the fields as we migrated around America. My daughter has heard about her father's legal work over three decades, representing migrant farmworkers and other poor people, work that at times resulted in threats to his life. She has been told how her father and I were made to sit in the back of a restaurant, and our subsequent successful effort to organize and force the passage of a city public accommodations ordinance forbidding such discrimination.

I have told her how I helped to organize an entire community against domestic violence, bringing about the adoption of new enforcement policies by the police and prosecutors. She (and her younger brother when he learns to read) will read pages of old press clippings and will be told many, many more stories about voting rights cases; involvement in organizations that sought to improve the status of women and children; marches for justice; and lawsuits challenging racism and sexism in the distribution of jobs, benefits, education, and services. She will learn of the constant efforts her parents and their friends undertook to improve their community and the world a bit.

Each time my daughter innocently declares that those were simply the bad old days, I will turn on the television, take her down to the courthouse, or buy her lunch with the local heads of the League United for Latin American Citizens, the League of Women Voters, and the National Association for the Advancement of Colored People. I will invite her to visit a migrant labor camp or give her some recent opinions from the courts and public comments from the Ku Klux Klan, skinheads, and talk-show hosts to read. I will instruct her not to forget history or ignore the current events around her.

During the course of my daughter's education in the history of her family and her country, I will also expose her to the basics of power and democracy, to politics in America. I want my daughter to understand that on the one hand, most people are primarily concerned about local problems, and thus political decisions should be those that best support and stabilize our families and communities. Politicians, on the other hand, oftentimes react to the money and power of lobbyists who seek only their clients' self-interest. Except in campaign speeches, politicians rarely concern themselves primarily with the interests of our families and neighborhoods; otherwise, our children's future would not be mortgaged. This open and obvious political conflict has not helped Americans of the 1990s to love and trust their elected politicians. Distrust is also fueled by the cynicism of many baby boomers, who remember being misled and lied to by politicians. Distrust is compounded in the voting booth when politics as usual means our choice is limited to the lesser of two evils as the best candidate.

I want my daughter to understand when she launches her first political campaign in the next century that a new kind of politician desperately will be needed—an honest, hardworking public servant.

Enumerating the problems in our system will not, however, overwhelm and dominate my education of my daughter. The system is flawed. Although it never will be perfect, it still is the best system in the world. It is possible in this country, and probably no other, to effect some real change if we put our minds to it.

We all know that politics is involved in everything from getting the garbage picked up to the response time of the fire department to passing a local public accommodations ordinance. After long and concerted efforts, all of us have experienced some successes—passage of the Occupational Health and Safety Act, Civil Rights and Voting Rights Acts, Clean Water and Clean Air Acts, Family Leave Act, and others. These are examples of national legislation that along with many state and local initiatives, bettered and made more secure the lives of many of us.

After we provide our daughters both a formal and a political education, what else is there to be done? Together, we need to ensure that democracy, not just politics as usual, wins the day by the time our daughters are ready to run for office. I believe we should work in three basic areas: political democracy, economic democracy, and exportation of democracy. Our work in these three general areas can take many forms.

POLITICAL DEMOCRACY

Free and fair elections are essential so that the will of the people can be reflected in government in every matter that is important in people's lives. Such elections involve more than simply allowing folks to vote. We must ensure that voting rights are not diminished; we must encourage aggressive enforcement of the Voting Rights Act by the Justice Department, civil rights organizations, and attorneys nationwide. Aggressive enforcement of the Voting Rights Act to date has directly resulted in more minorities, and I believe more women, being elected to public office.

The election of more women and minorities also has been aided in part by objective voter forums sponsored around the country by the League of Women Voters to educate the public about the credentials and qualifications, other than money, of the candidates. In some areas, the league has also assisted in the litigation of voting rights cases by gathering information and funding the cases. All our efforts with local Leagues of Women Voters and other voluntary organizations must continue.

Who controls the wealth in this country and to whom do these people give money in the primaries and elections? In other words, as we learned during Watergate, follow the money. The right to vote is diminished when our choice of possible candidates is controlled by a process that is heavily dependent upon money. The distortion of the political process by our campaign finance laws has been well documented. The current way we fund elections creates unreasonable hurdles for women and minorities to clear in order to be elected, hurdles that public debates sponsored by the league cannot offset. All of us have seen an election or legislation turn on a few votes. The plain truth is that the people who gain the politician's ear when critical votes are cast are not individuals but lobbyists with money and clout and organized groups that can deliver votes, money, or threats. We must continue to push for campaign finance reform, lobbyist reform, and the vigorous prosecution of those who violate the law.

Some say the Congress is the largest exclusive club in this country. A similar exclusivity is reflected in many state legislatures, city councils, and school boards. Are there ways to end that exclusivity so that others can run and win public office? Although three generations have passed since women won the right to vote, the expected diversity among elected officials has not materialized.

Before another generation goes by, we must devise electoral policies that fine-tune our democracy, enabling the broader participation and inclusion of women and minorities (who make up the majority of this country's population). Whether it is through government funding of candidates and other campaign finance reforms or through innovative electoral experiments, we must admit that, unless we act to change it, the system will continue as is. Other changes, such as creating single-member electoral districts, have already produced dramatic opportunities for minority voters to have an impact on the outcome of elections and for minority candidates to win positions in our local and state governments.

Over the years, through my law firm's activities in voting rights litigation, I have been involved in the establishment of single-member districts as a witness, a fundraiser for a civil rights organization, a plaintiff, and a board member of the Mexican American Legal Defense and Education Fund (MALDEF). Each of us must choose a level at which we can effectively participate while we continue to establish single-member districts as one very effective method of diversifying and stimulating local elections.

Equal access to the judicial branch is even more problematic than equal access to the legislative branch. Providing equal access to the judicial system hinges on more than simply adopting fair and free elections. Rising legal costs are making each person's right to her or his day in court before a jury of her or his peers prohibitively expensive for the middle class. For the poor, equal access is almost impossible unless they are provided an attorney from a typically understaffed local legal aid or public defender's office.

During my six years as an assistant state attorney general in West Texas and my subsequent years in private practice across the plains of West Texas and an island off the Texas coast, I witnessed a steady stream of families in desperate need of affordable legal representation. A justice system that excludes entire classes of people is doomed to become irrelevant in their lives. The feminization of poverty over the last two decades in this country of laws means that poor women and their children who are struggling each day to simply survive are especially hard hit as a group when they are unable to enforce the laws in their favor or to defend themselves. Our mothers, sisters, and daughters deserve better.

One branch of government cannot continue to be out of reach of large segments of the people of this country. Real efforts must be undertaken, not just lip service, to ensure equal access to justice in this country. Otherwise we must be ready to accept the probable continued increase of lawless solutions.

As one of President Clinton's appointees to the board of the Legal Services Corporation, I have studied various methods of ensuring that justice in civil cases is not pocketbook justice, that access is not solely dependent upon the marketplace. I believe a hybrid system of quality professional legal aid offices working with court-appointed private attorneys and local pro bono programs must be created and adequately funded. Effective methods of encouraging more participation from the private bar must also be developed. Another part of the solution is to create a greater number of effective alternative dispute resolution centers around the country—justice does not always have to come in the form of a decision from a judge in a black robe.

After participating in our legal system for nearly twenty years, I have concluded that all of us must undertake a long-term effort to end the hostility in our society and restore some basic civility and manners. Our country is probably the most litigious and violent on earth. Our courthouses are filled with legal gunslingers and folks looking for a hired gun to fight for them. Our democracy and society cannot be a positive model if "Getting mine and getting even" is the motto, as opposed to "Let's make sure it doesn't happen again, and let's work together." While we must ensure equal and fair access to our justice system for all Americans, the present pattern of resolving every dispute through a slugfest in the courts or the streets instead of around a table cannot remain our accepted practice. Both civil wars and civil litigation wars waste the time, energy, and resources of society, and both create casualties.

Perhaps as more of our daughters graduate from law schools, attitudes will change from endorsing Rambo-style litigation and destruction of opposing parties to promoting diplomacy and peacemaking with our neighbors. It is clear to me which is more likely to build a tolerant democratic society.

ECONOMIC DEMOCRACY

Improving the legislative and judicial branches of government is important and will go a long way toward making our lives and our democracy better. We should also consider, however, whether those same fundamental democratic ideals that all of us embrace should also apply to other areas of our society.

We want the principles of access and participation to apply when our government makes decisions about fundamental issues like war, taxes, education, abortion, child support, health care, and social security. It is possible that these principles should also frame the democratic models for other important areas of our daily lives.

For generations, the government has regulated monopolies and enacted taxes, tariffs, zoning requirements, and restrictions about what and where things could be manufactured, sold, and dumped. The government became involved in various aspects of our free enterprise system to meet our need to balance the competing interests of business, consumers, the general public, and working families.

This country is not the same as it was when it was founded. Today large and powerful entities have dramatic effects on our lives. Many of America's most important decisions are made not in our elected legislatures but in corporate boardrooms. The operations of some enterprises are regulated by the Federal Trade Commission and the Securities and Exchange Commission and by such laws as the Fair Housing Act, the Community Reinvestment Act, and the Environmental Protection Act. But most of the time, these laws seem to be far too little and always many years too late. I suspect that the lobbyists for these entities and the desires of incumbent politicians for reelection interfere with more timely action.

Therefore, I think citizen participation to influence decisions that affect our lives should move beyond the legislature and other political bodies. Thoughtful public-minded individuals should be encouraged to involve themselves in the decision-making processes of corporate entities that have an impact on our lives. People can become involved at the shareholder level or strive to become members of boards of directors. Once a corporation is identified as having a significant impact on the state's interest in the health, safety, or welfare of the people, it may be appropriate to require the placement of a public representative on the board of directors as a corporate condition of doing business. The representative would be responsible for representing the public's interest rather than the corporation's profit margin.

Decisions and actions concerning product safety, working conditions, wages, the retraining of workers, health insurance, campaign contributions, lobbying activities, environmental concerns, and plant relocation all may change when the public concerns of the community are expressed and debated alongside the private interests of the directors and shareholders.

EXPORTATION OF DEMOCRACY

Our efforts to expand democracy at home should be joined by our continuing efforts to expand it around the world. It is in our national interest to spread democracy, especially in this hemisphere, where our country's historical support of undemocratic governments is legendary.

The transfer of power through elections is superior to opposing parties' shooting it out. Civil war and unrest waste the lives of mostly civilian noncombatants—women and children. They waste resources. They waste the time of farmers who could be planting and of schoolteachers who could be preparing the next generation. They often involve the United States because we may send advisers, troops, money, and weapons to one side or the other.

The underlying principles of the Declaration of Independence, which freed us from King George III to pursue government, as Abraham Lincoln later said, "of the people, by the people, and for the people," will benefit all people living under undemocratic governments. Exporting democracy does not mean that we should impose our way of life upon other people. Certainly, however, our efforts to assist those countries through governmental and private efforts should continue to be tied as much as possible to democratic reforms and promotion of human rights. When requested, we should participate with other international observers to ensure that elections are fair.

In 1993, I participated in a series of discussions and meetings held around this country and Mexico concerning the North American Free Trade Agreement (NAFTA). While no one is entirely pleased with that treaty, it is clear that our future is closely linked with Mexico's. We must participate in efforts to create economic stability and establish democracy within Mexico and points south. Failure to do so could lead to future U.S. policies and actions with severe negative consequences, especially for Hispanics and working people.

My daughter will need to know and understand the significance of the following fact: by the year 2000, about 20 percent of the U.S. population will be of Latin American and Caribbean origin, making the United States the fifth largest Latin American country in the world. Already some of the largest Hispanic "cities" in the world exist in sections of the largest cities of the United States.

As an elected Hispanic politician in the twenty-first century, one of my daughter's obligations will be to ensure that the viewpoints of Hispanics are listened to when issues concerning this hemisphere are publicly, or privately, considered. She will encourage corporations to include Hispanics at the negotiating table and in the boardroom. She will argue that business as usual is no longer acceptable; our southern neighbors and relatives deserve our respect and good faith as we work together to develop vibrant free democracies.

CONCLUSION

The American Revolution and the U.S. Constitution are bright shining points in the history of the world. Our government, however, was not set in stone two hundred years ago. We have amended the Constitution many times to protect the rights of the people and make our democracy more perfect. We placed term limits on the presidency to avoid the possibility of a future imperial president. We protected our right to protest and speak out against the government. And we finally understood that the majority of us in this country should have the right to vote.

In order to create a more perfect union, we must continue to change. We must experiment. We must be prepared to reject the old ways when they no longer work and, after experimenting with new ideas locally, statewide, and nationally, back off from those ideas that fail. Although we need to reinvent our government every so often, we do not need to reinvent democracy. It simply needs to be aggressively protected and to have its basic virtues of access and participation encouraged at every level and in every corner of our society.

I believe democracy is not just about being able to elect a new and different person to a public office; it is also about the ability of those elected representatives to adopt and implement different policies. If real change cannot be accomplished by our elected representatives because they are responding to powerful and narrow special interests, then we do not have a meaningful democracy.

In the end, it will not matter whether my daughter is elected president if she is the leader of a country that has failed to preserve the real promise of democracy. Without a strong democracy, whatever real change may be needed in her future will not happen; our country's future will then be in the hands of the powerful few, not of the people. Those of us who want the possibility of real change always to be available must continue our efforts to increase, broaden, and protect our democracy. Our daughters and sons deserve our best efforts.

NANCY Y. BEKAVAC is president of Scripps College. She is a
former partner in the law firm of Munger, Tolles and Olson and
was executive director of the Thomas J. Watson Foundation from
1985 to 1987. From 1988 to 1990, she was counselor to the
president of Dartmouth College. Bekavac is a member of
the Committee on Women in Higher Education of the American
Council on Education, the Advisory Council of WOMENS-
WORK, and the Executive Committee of the Association
of Independent California Colleges and Universities. A graduate
of Swarthmore College and Yale Law School, she serves on
the board of managers of Swarthmore College.

Imagining the
Real Future

Nancy Y. Bekavac

*E*ver since I became president of Scripps College in 1990, I
have been privileged to view women's participation in politics
from a particular vantage point. At Scripps, a women's residential liberal arts college in Southern California, I speak daily with women
whose collegiate experience by and large coincides with their eligibility
to vote as well as with their initial experience of living away from their
families.

The first five years of the 1990s marked a tumultuous time in American politics: we experienced the collapse of the Soviet Union, the Gulf
War, continued debates over abortion funding and access, the presidential election of 1992, and the "Republican Revolution" of the 1994
congressional election. In California, we also experienced the civil unrest in Los Angeles after the acquittal of police defendants in the Rodney King trial. Moreover, several highly controversial issues were

placed on the ballot in the state, especially those dealing with the treatment of illegal immigrants and with affirmative action. For young women, particularly in Southern California, these are challenging and often confusing times.

Seventy-five years after passage of the constitutional amendment guaranteeing American women the right to vote, the members of the new generation of women clearly feel confident in their potential to be effective and full citizens of the United States. I cannot hope to speak for these young women; they speak eloquently enough for themselves. But I would like to pass along some of my observations as a member of the baby boomer generation about the experiences and possibilities the women in this new generation will carry into their political maturity and about some of their shared assumptions. Their experiences are sufficiently different from those of the baby boomers and the generations preceding them to give us pause in inferring a clear and certain future. Two sets of incidents will demonstrate the source of my concerns.

The first took place during discussions in the residence halls on the third or fourth day of the Gulf War. A small group of students, mostly Caucasian but including Chicanas, African Americans, and Asian Americans, gathered for a discussion about the war with the dean of faculty and me. Their opinions on the war ranged from fervent support to dismay, confusion, and outright opposition. A number of these students asked about the prospects of conscription—one in particular was concerned about her brother. She did not know, and seemed surprised to learn, that Congress had abolished the draft nearly twenty years before, retaining only vestigial draft registration requirements for men.

I was also intrigued by these young women's reactions to what I viewed as one of the most startling aspects of the Gulf War: the deployment of American women military personnel to frontline "support" positions (although what constituted "frontline" was sometimes a difficult issue in this high-tech conflict). I had been particularly struck by the newspaper and television images showing mothers of young children leaving for the war while the fathers held crying infants and talked about assuming child care and other responsibilities. When I asked the students what they thought of these images, they seemed a bit surprised. "They're soldiers. It's their duty; they're trained for it," was the general tone of the replies.

I pressed the issue further, remembering vividly the conundrum of women who loved men—brothers, friends, boyfriends—who faced the draft during the Vietnam War and our coming to terms with the paradox of our own immunity from the threat of conscription, an immunity almost never questioned by anyone in all the endless debates about that war. "Aren't mothers needed at home in a different way than fathers?" I asked. "How would you feel if you were called up and your brothers weren't?" The young women seemed untouched by these questions. Finally, I asked, "Suppose Congress reintroduced the draft. How would you feel about a draft for men and women?" "Fine," they all said. "We vote; we're citizens. It isn't fair to require men to do what we don't have to do." End of discussion.

When I told them that federal law does not require women to register for the draft, they shrugged. When I told them that federal law explicitly bars women from serving in combat, they simply could not dredge up any interest anymore than they wanted to debate bustles or corsets (well, maybe corsets—Madonna was in her bustier phase at the time). I had essentially the same discussion four or five times that spring term, including a discussion with some high school seniors who visited the campus.

All of these women, in the spring of 1991, took as an established principle the idea that women bear not only equal but *identical* burdens as citizens, including that responsibility explicitly denied by federal law: to serve equally in their nation's defense in battle.

All of these women grew up during the 1980s when, at least according to many surveys and commentaries, women's rights and advocacy decreased. Moreover, the country failed to ratify the Equal Rights Amendment. Yet these students' deeply rooted conception of their place in the center of national debate and national service was shaped during that same period. Indeed, they formed a conclusion that only the most radical theorists of the 1960s advocated: women have identical rights and obligations in national defense as well as in every other aspect of citizenship.

I believe that such deep assumptions—that women belong in the military, that their family obligations are no different or more special than men's obligations, that the ultimate call of the nation for service in wartime must be met in the same way by both men and women, both single and married people—ultimately will guide this generation's responses to major political issues over time, particularly to the issue of women's right to lead, not just follow, in the public sphere. The older view of women as auxiliaries to men's enterprises was hallowed by tradition and culture; it is found in the federal law that relegates women to military "support" services. I would say that older view has little future.

In retrospect, we can see that some part of the debate over women's leadership in the antiwar and even in the civil rights struggle of the 1960s turned on unspoken assumptions about women's immunity from dangerous service. Denied the opportunity for heroism in battle abroad or in the streets, women were also denied the opportunity for leadership in politics.

Now those assumptions seem to be falling away like the traditional belief that women's proper sphere lies solely in domestic life and emotional nurturing. With the new assumptions comes an unwillingness to face unpleasant facts that run contrary to these young women's views and values—facts like the law relegating women to supporting and therefore secondary roles in the military, an imperfect analogy to the old vision of wives remaining at home while they see their soldier husbands off to war.

A second event reinforces what I believe is the younger generation's definitively altered view of women's possibilities in public life. On election night 1992, Scripps College set up a very large television screen in an auditorium so that the members of the college community could watch the election results together. We had popcorn and cocoa, blackboards with running totals, and announcements of winners in our own contests for the Scripps class with the highest voter registration percentage and the highest voter turnout. Several faculty and staff along with the usual complement of children, dogs, neighbors, and other passersby were there, a varying crowd of two or three hundred during the course of the evening.

Looking around at a group that was perhaps 75 to 85 percent women, I realized that in all my previous election night vigils, I never had been with so overwhelmingly female a crowd. I knew from the college's comparative data on student attitudes that Scripps students are more idealistic and politically more liberal than their collegiate counterparts generally. So it was no surprise that they cheered most of the early returns showing a Democratic tide. What was striking, however, was the sisterly solidarity that kept welling up. The crowd responded anxiously, and then enthusiastically, as results from the "Year of the Woman" scrolled across the screen. I particularly remember a sophomore calling out, "I'm from Illinois—I voted for her!" when Carol Moseley-Braun's name blinked on in victory. Women cheered as various returns and predictions were entered on the large maps, but the loudest cheer of all came when the ticker along the bottom of the screen projected Barbara Boxer as well as Dianne Feinstein winning senatorial seats in California—the first time in history any state had elected two women to the U.S. Senate. The reaction was electric; young women danced and hugged and cheered wildly. They stood on chairs and waved. Clearly they felt some part of the victory and some measure of vindication.

The news of California's double election of woman Senators came just as the television cameras were trained on the stage in Little Rock, awaiting candidates Clinton and Gore and their wives. Shortly after the four emerged into the spotlight, Bill Clinton turned to his wife and whispered something. Partly because the projected television image was so large, we all clearly saw her take a piece of paper from her pocket and hand it to him; it was from that piece of paper that he spoke. What he said at first was lost in a roar of young women standing up on chairs cheering, not necessarily for President-elect Clinton but for first-lady-to-be Hillary Rodham Clinton. The women were shouting, in unison, "*She* wrote it! *She* wrote it! *She* wrote it!"

I was truly surprised by the reactions—ambushed, as it were, by the passions and emotions I had seen on a campus and during an election that had not seemed particularly involving for the students, even though our surveys showed that more than half of them had registered and voted. Their reactions to women's elections were probably foreseeable, but I was astonished at the reaction to the scene in Little Rock. I saw in that incident a brief insight of intimate partnership, even of wifely dutifulness. The students "read" the clues differently, inferring authorship from Mrs. Clinton's possession of the paper and probably interpreting the relationship differently as well.

Having grown up in the placid 1950s and then matured in the turbulent 1960s, I hold very different assumptions about men and women, I suppose. And having spent my own college years during the riveting, bitter debates of American involvement in Vietnam, I could be systematically disabled from seeing or understanding what politics and elections mean to these women, whose first political lessons were learned in the climate fostered by Watergate.

After the last of the concession speeches, I walked back to my house on campus, marveling at what I had seen on those faces and heard in those voices of Scripps women at the beginning of their voting lives. They had a wholly new set of expectations and ambitions: they had just seen, and many had voted for, women elected in record numbers to high office. These students would begin their political maturity expecting not just to be active politically but to see themselves and their fellow students as candidates, as major forces in politics, as Senators and political advisers and forces in their own right.

How different their experience would be from mine. I began my political education watching my mother argue with the television set during the McCarthy-Army Hearings in 1954; there was not a woman on the screen. The first elections I remember were my uncle's campaigns for mayor of our small town in western Pennsylvania. My first vote was cast in the Pennsylvania primary of 1968, in which Governor George

Wallace made a surprisingly strong showing against Hubert Humphrey and Eugene McCarthy. My first general election vote came that November, when many of my dispirited friends cast symbolic votes for noncandidates or refused to vote at all given a choice between Richard M. Nixon and Hubert H. Humphrey. No women were on either the primary or general election ballot. Certainly I would not have thought of running for office as an option to emulate, even though I thought of myself as fully enfranchised.

In the years after my first vote, I stayed active as a financial contributor, sometime campaign worker, and consistent voter, but many years passed before I had the chance to vote for women candidates seeking high office. I have watched women candidates and officeholders criticized, as their male colleagues and opponents are not, for their clothing and hairstyles and hem lines, for child care and homemaking arrangements, for slips of temper that are commonplace in the masculine world, for daring to speak on topics that some contend are "off limits" to women, and for failing to speak on topics that are "supposed" to be women's issues. Because I know and admire some of these women, I wince and worry and wonder how such biases can be overcome.

Scripps students, by and large, assume these differences do not matter; the differences are unimportant in their view of the world. These young women seem to be blinded or, better yet, looking at facts through polarized lenses that filter out what they do not want to see. While calmly asserting belief in a radical social and political equality, they seem oblivious, or indifferent, to actual inequities: federal laws affecting the military, the gender pay differential in the marketplace, the complex expectations for first ladies, or the double burdens of family and work that women bear every day.

Nevertheless, I hope these Scripps women are not terribly different in their aspirations and assumptions from women their age across the country and across the political spectrum. Almost a century and a half after they helped to mold the abolitionist movement into a great political force, and half again as long after they gained the constitutional right to vote, women are beginning to merge into the electorate and the ranks of political candidates not as valorous heroines or moral avenging angels, not even as political heiresses to great family names or fortunes, but as workaday everyday politicians of pluck and hard work and occasional grandeur.

The women who will dominate the politics of the next fifty to seventy-five years will emerge over the next few years much as other candidates do. And younger women assume these future candidates will experience neither the special barrier of explaining that a woman can do the job nor the special benefits of automatic support because of their gender.

That is, for better or worse (and I must believe it is for better), the legacy of the last seventy-five years. It is the legacy of the women who proposed and campaigned for universal suffrage, and those who took advantage of suffrage to become leaders not just of women but of the nation. Women like Jeannette Rankin, Frances Perkins, Eleanor Roosevelt, Margaret Chase Smith, Rosa Parks, Shirley Chisholm, and Barbara Jordan come to mind. Today's female officeholders are their beneficiaries, who in turn will mark the transition to a new generation that will make the 19th Amendment not so much a signpost as a memorial along a much traveled highway.

The young women who have helped me to understand the interior landscape of assumptions and values on which they map their plans and lives showed me how much has changed from our maps of twenty-five years ago. These women expect, like a friend's daughter who is ten, that by the time they are ready to campaign, they will not be seeking to become the first woman president of the United States but the third or fourth. While their experiences to date have given them a set of assumptions and values far more radically egalitarian, and optimistic, than my generation's, I worry for them.

For all of us, I believe, women's political activity is a given; our leadership at all but the highest levels is now accepted. What remains is the consolidation and normalization of women's leadership and values—not because women are "as good as" men but because these leaders are good women, as different from men as men are different from women, as similar to men as men are similar to women and both necessary to humanity.

I believe that many Scripps students underestimate the difficulties that remain; they think I am a victim of old fears. At my most optimistic, I hope they are engaged in that creative enterprise Martin Buber called "imagining the real"—imagining desired goals to shape our actions in a purposeful way so that through our actions, we make those goals concrete. I hope this is what I am seeing, because this is what the world needs so desperately: the informed passions, involvement, talents, genius, and ideals of all of our citizens. That is the goal toward which woman suffrage has helped to move our nation.

THE EDITOR

NANCY M. NEUMAN was national president of the League of Women Voters from 1986 to 1990. A lecturer and writer on women in politics and public policy, she is a former distinguished visiting professor at Washington and Jefferson College (1991 and 1994), Bucknell University (1992), and Pomona College (1990). Neuman is also a Woodrow Wilson Visiting Fellow. She received a B.A. degree from Pomona College and an M.A. degree in political science from the University of California at Berkeley. She holds honorary doctorates from Pomona College and Westminster College.

Neuman is president of the Pennsylvania Women's Campaign Fund. A public member of the American Bar Association Accreditation Committee, she served in Pennsylvania on the Disciplinary Board of the Supreme Court, the Judicial Inquiry and Review Board, and the Federal Judicial Nominating Commission, which she chaired. Active in housing policy and civil rights, Neuman is a board member and former president of the national Housing Assistance Council and served on the Leadership Conference on Civil Rights, the Pennsylvania Housing Finance Agency, and the Federal Home Loan Bank of Pittsburgh.

A former president of her state and local Leagues of Women Voters, Neuman chaired the league's national ERA ratification campaign for three years. She is the author of *The League of Women Voters in Perspective: 1920–1995* (1994).

INDEX

Photography Credits

Nancy Y. Bekavac: © S. Peter Lopez

Barbara Davis Blum: © Dunn Photographic Associates, Inc.

Corinne C. "Lindy" Boggs: © 1995 George Long/Longshots

Mary Chapin Carpenter: Caroline Greyshock / © 1995 Sony Music Entertainment

Rosalynn Carter: "Women Who Shaped the Constitution," © Wayne Perkins; "Challenges and Change in One Woman's Life," © Rick Diamond Photography

Hillary Rodham Clinton: official White House photo

Ada E. Deer: courtesy of Lydia Bickford and Jon Holtshopple

Betty Ford: © Douglas Kirkland

Elisabeth Griffith: © Frank M. Lavelle

Beverly J. Harvard: © Atlanta Police Department

Bernadine Healy: courtesy Bernadine Healy

Antonia Hernández: © George Rodriguez

Nicole Hollander: © Jennifer Girard Photographer

Gwen Ifill: © Gwen Ifill/NBC News

Wilma P. Mankiller: © 1996 Wilma P. Mankiller

Sarah McClendon: © 1995 Christy Bowe

Mary Adelia Rosamond McLeod: © Gillian Randall Photography

Sara E. Meléndez: © Day Walters

Maria Luisa Mercado: © Victor Mosqueda Photography, Inc.

Martina Navratilova: © Greg Gorman

Esther Peterson: Murray Bognovitz / © Abstract Studios, Inc.

Condoleezza Rice: © Stanford News Service

Lucinda Desha Robb: © Leslie Cashen

Anne Firor Scott: © Les Todd/Duke University Photography

Donna Shalala: © Len DePas

Rebecca Walker: © JoAnne Savio

Judy Woodruff: © Cable News Network, Inc. All rights reserved.

Diane C. Yu: © Max Ramirez